Mindful Athletic Performance

Winning the Game
On and Off the Field

Table of Contents

Foreword

My whole life, I was an athlete. I played football, basketball and baseball in high school and went to William and Mary on a football scholarship. After college, I played professional football overseas, which was when I got injured. Looking back, it's easy to see how that injury became a game-changing moment in my life. Although it meant that I was no longer going be a professional-level athlete, it also led me to the realization that I wanted to work with athletes. Today I work with some of the world's best athletes including NFL MVPs, MLB and NBA All-Stars, Super Bowl champions and Olympic gold medalists.

Onc of the things I learned as I recovered from that injury was that mindset means everything. Getting your mind right is what allows you to overcome any adversity. It's what led me to discover that a setback does not need to define you. Instead a setback can actually become a setup. In my case, that injury set me up to live my life purpose, which is to create, motivate and inspire people to greatness.

Whether I am working with athletes, business owners, executives or leaders in their field, one defining trait of anyone who wants to reach their optimal potential is that they have the mindset of a champion. That means they are focused on what they want to achieve, and they do whatever it takes to make it happen. In other words, they consistently work to get 1% better – *every single day*! They do that by surrounding themselves with positivity, visualizing their goals, following their purpose, and doing simple things like reading books that motivate and inspire them.

Because you are holding this book in your hands I can see that you, too, are ready to be inspired. The fact that you've opened these pages shows me you have a growth mindset and are looking to get better in your life. So, let me tell you a little bit about what you are going to read.

This book is written by eight fitness professionals who train both the 'Joes' and the pros. Through their experience, they have learned what it takes to create champions – whether you are playing on the field or off. In these pages, you are going to read their stories and discover their secrets to becoming a top performer, whether you are a youth athlete, a professional athlete, or anyone in between. They are going to show you that being an athlete goes way beyond sets and reps. It is about being your best, digging deep and unleashing the power you have within.

Are you ready to do that?

Then it's time to start reading. Allow these stories to move, inspire and motivate you. Take notes. Re-read the sections that resonate with you. There are many lessons to be learned, and I want you to absorb all of them as you read.

Keeping growing, keep learning, and continue to empower yourself.

And most of all, *Get Your Mind Right* so you can go out and live your best life!

Much love and much STRENGTH,

Todd Durkin, MA, CSCS
Owner, Fitness Quest 10
Under Armour Training Team
Author, ***The IMPACT Body Plan*** and ***The WOW Book***

Chapter 1

The 7 Pillars of Youth Athletics: Preparing for Something More Important Than Sports – Adult Life

By Greg Justice, MA

The debate over youth sports and the benefit and harm for the kids and young adults involved has been going on for a long time. However, some things cannot be debated, such as the certain impact that they have on individuals later on in their adult years. People who participated in youth sports when they were young were exposed to one of the world's greatest catalysts for growth and change. In sports, they learned to become better teammates, trained themselves to be faster and stronger, and gradually gained discipline as they went through hours of practice. While these skills and personality traits were vitally important to becoming a better athlete, they became even more important in adult life. Although they were focused solely on the sport at the time, individuals participating in youth sports were subconsciously practicing for something even more important than sports: adult life.

Participation in youth sports helps shape the whole person into a better version of his or herself, but the changes and growth that occur can be combined and categorized into several areas. Each of these areas will be explained and expanded upon in detail later in this chapter. Before reading, however, it is important to highlight that the particular sport the individual participated in does not change the existence of these areas. However, some sports do foster the growth of certain areas more than others. For example, wrestlers learn that discipline is vital to success, whereas cross-country runners have more development in perseverance. The bench system of basketball increases basketball players' growth in the understanding of structure, while football players are forced to develop teamwork skills to the extreme. The nature of the game itself plays a major role in the rate at which some characteristics develop. However, some traits are independent of any sport the individual played in. Goal setting and good habits are needed no matter what sport you play, and respect is something highly emphasized in all youth sports at all levels. The various rates of development based on what sport the person played is an interesting phenomenon, but more important is the final combination of these major skills that help mold the player into a better person as they move on to and through adult life.

Pillar #1: Teamwork

You may have been able to guess that teamwork would appear near the top of the list. This is no coincidence. Teamwork is a vital skill that is used every single day. Whether it is at work, in family life, or during sports, teamwork is crucial to achieving the lofty goals we set for ourselves. Historical evidence and studies suggest that humans are not wired to survive on our own and that we need cooperation and coordination with others to reach our full potential.

Youth sports and all sports by nature are team-driven activities. Whether players on a team must work together simultaneously to play (i.e., football, basketball) or members of a team contribute individually to the team's overall result (i.e., wrestling, track), they are a team nonetheless. This teaches players that they alone are not able to accomplish greatness or the amount of success that they wish to achieve without the help and support of others. It is important to note that this lesson is taught in a positive way. Players are not taught to feel bad because they are not good enough, but rather to accept that they need help along the way in order to succeed in some tasks. In adult life this is true in many cases. Try and find a career where your work is independent of anyone else, a company where you sit in an office without interacting with others to achieve a common goal. To save you the time, we'll give you a hint: you can't find one.

In essence, teamwork is the process of building trust, unity, and making the group more efficient while trying to reach a common goal. From the time a child first plays sports, all the way through high school and even college, there is an emphasis on the "team first" mindset. While in the real world it is important to focus on personal goals as well, participation in youth sports helps to instill the mindset needed to work well in teams later in life. Compared to someone that didn't participate in sports and was not engaged in this mindset from an early age, sports players have a huge advantage. Being comfortable working in a team environment and thriving in it rather than suffering through it is a trait that takes time to develop. Developing it through sports from a young age is a true head start that helps set the individual up for success later in life.

Teamwork is all around us, and while you may dread the group presentation or team sales pitch, knowing how to be in and work in this environment is still a crucial and constant part of adult life. Through participation in team sports at a young age, these skills are developed and lead to a better team member as an adult. Despite its tremendous importance, teamwork is only one area of the person that is developed by youth sports. Many others also contribute to help make a more well-rounded adult.

Pillar #2: Respect

Respect is a hot topic in society today. Despite how strange that sentence sounds, it holds true for everyone. Respect for people in the workplace, those in differing social demographics and those of different age groups are all topics seen in the news on a regular basis. Although teens are often given a bad rap for being disrespectful, respect is a topic that many adults could use some work on. However, we again see how youth sports help to build a culture of respect among its participants and how this mindset carries on into adult life. In sports, players are taught respect in four general areas. Each of these areas translates in some way and in some degree to adult life. At least one of these areas is typically difficult for people to grasp for one reason or another, but by being repeatedly encouraged to show respect in all of them through sports, the individual has a much greater overall respect.

To make any sport happen, there must be people. Coaches, players, and referees all come together to make it happen. Sports are something that helps bring together people from all different backgrounds to enjoy an activity together. This all happens through respect. The first area of respect that youth sports teach is respect for the individuals that are a part of it. Players are taught to respect their coaches and teammates. A team cannot hope to perform on the field if they quarrel amongst themselves and disrespect each other. To have a solid team, there must be a solid foundation. Players are also taught to respect the opposing team's players. This, while difficult at times, creates a safe environment to play in without things becoming personal or violent. Finally, players are taught to respect the referees, officials, or judges. Many times, the player may not agree with the call or penalty, but they are taught to show respect for the referee and accept it without throwing a fit on the field (something that many professional players do a poor job of modeling). This foundation of respect for other people is of supreme importance in adult life. Without respecting those around us, we soon lose their respect for us, and therefore struggle through life with a poor reputation and a lack of friends.

Sports also teach us that the game we choose to play and love is a privilege. Each time we take field, we honor the legacies of those who have come before us and set the bar for those that will come after us. Being involved in youth sports teaches us to respect the sport we take part in. We are taught to be content with the activity we are taking part in and to treat it with respect by acting in a professional and appropriate manner. As we progress into adult life, the sport is replaced somewhat by a more general situation. Whether that is a job, an economic status, or any other situation, this tradition of respect carries over. People who take part in youth sports are more likely to respect their current situation, rather than being disgruntled by it.

Similarly, players are taught to have respect for the outcome regardless of what it is. If the team loses, an individual goal isn't met, or any other adverse event occurs, we are by nature unhappy with it. While it is okay to be disappointed or unhappy, it is also important to still have respect for the outcome. This is true for adult life as well, in many ways. Maybe you didn't get the promotion, or the house you wanted to buy was sold before you could make an offer. Despite being upset about these things, it is important to still respect the outcome in a civil way.

The final area of respect taught though sports is respect for yourself. Without this, respect in the other three areas is very difficult to achieve. Sports teach us that we are all unique and have a set of talents and abilities that make us special. In this way we learn to respect ourselves and avoid falling into the trap of self-dislike that ensnares many people in our society. By learning to respect ourselves from a young age, this mindset carries through into the adult years and makes the individual more confident, happy, and motivated.

Pillar #3: Discipline

Something that goes hand-in-hand with respect is discipline. In fact, as one develops, so does the other. These two traits are both extremely important in sports and in adult life. Much like respect, there are several areas of discipline that come about through participation in youth sports. Each of these is important in their own right and help to accomplish different things. Development of physical, mental, and emotional discipline all occur through participation in youth sports and help one to have a better overall adult life.

Perhaps the most obvious form of discipline that comes to mind when thinking of sports is physical discipline. This refers to the countless hours put into training, drills, conditioning, and everything else that athletes do every day in practice. Establishing this physical discipline is a crucial part in becoming a good athlete, regardless of which sport you take part in. However, the process of learning to physically discipline yourself extends even further than just working out. It also includes eating well and getting enough sleep. This is the way in which it carries over into adult life. As adults, we are all too often too caught up in the hustle and bustle of our daily routine to remember to eat healthy, and unfortunately, sleep seems to become a secondary priority. However, if we have been disciplined from a young age to do so, it is much easier to continue doing so in later years.

The second form of discipline evolved from youth sports participation is mental discipline. While this is a very broad description, it generally means keeping yourself in check mentally throughout your daily activities. This includes focusing on the task at hand, staying motivated, and forcing yourself to do what you need to do even if it isn't what you want to do at the moment. These activities obviously correlate into adult life in nearly every way possible.

Finally, sports teach us emotional discipline in difficult times. This is the slowest form of discipline to develop, but one of the most useful. In life, there are many situations that don't go our way. While this is natural and necessary, it does not ease the sting when it happens. However, by participating in sports, we are exposed to disappointment and heartbreak regularly, but in a safe environment where there are no real damages done because of it. Although there are no damages, the pain of the defeat is just as real, because of the time and dedication poured in. This teaches us to handle emotional hardship and to heal and grow stronger because of it. By becoming disciplined emotionally, we learn how to handle hard times and not allow them to control us or cause us to react out of character.

The development of these various forms of discipline all combine to cumulate in an all-around disciplined and stable person. Without participating in youth sports, there is significantly less exposure and less opportunity to grow in this way. Once again, compared to people who did not take part in sports during their developmental years, those who did take part possess these skills at a much higher rate.

Pillar #4: Structure

This category is partially determined by which sport is being played, but structure is a vital part of all sports. Without structure, it's just a game of backyard football or a pick-up game of basketball. Structure is the very thing that organizes the players and coaches and applies rules to the game that help make it what it is. However, structure is not something that is limited to the world of sports. It is a major component of the global and domestic job industry and every company and corporation has their own take on structure. Maybe there is one CEO, several managers, employees of a higher level, and then entry-level employees. Perhaps there is one owner and everyone else has the same status. Regardless of how the organization is structured, it must be understood and respected for everything to work correctly. Participation in sports helps to develop this understanding and enables people to do so in adulthood.

Sports such as football, baseball, soccer, basketball, generally considered team sports, specifically teach a hierarchical system in which coaches are at the top, followed by upperclassmen (usually captains), and then the rest of the team members. This system represents the traditional workplace. As mentioned above, there is a boss, some higher-level employees and then everyone else. Note that this is an extremely simplified explanation and that a real company is structured with many tiers and levels. However, the basic concepts are the same. For our purposes, the comparison is equivalent. This structure relies heavily on respect and consistency to make things work. With each game (ignoring injuries) the structure remains the same. The same coaches, captains, and players play in the same positions each time. This is very similar to the traditional workplace where each day generally consists of the same type of activities being done by the same people.

Other sports like cross-country, track, and wrestling, generally considered more individual sports, have a very fluid structure that can change day to day. There is still a coach in charge, but below him/her the players are generally equal, and determine their position on the team based on ability and skill. A runner in a varsity spot one week can easily be replaced by another runner not on varsity who ran a faster time. A varsity wrestler can be replaced by losing a pre-meet wrestle-off with another teammate in the same weight class. This structure helps the team ensure that its best athletes take the field each time to optimize the chances of success. In comparison to the workplace, this structure is something being seen more and more with small companies and start-ups. Specifically, in Silicon Valley, companies organize their employees into small teams where there are rotating "lead developers" or by projects where the current best get put to work while others take care of more mundane everyday tasks. While structures like this are highly efficient, they are still somewhat rare to see in practice, although they are spreading rapidly from the tech industry into other areas.

Regardless of which structure the athlete is exposed to and adjusts to, they get the key benefit of learning to adjust to and work in a structured environment. Those who participated in multiple sports and ones with different organizational structures benefit from even more diverse exposure. All of this helps individuals that participated in athletics make an easier transition into the workplace.

Pillar #5: Perseverance

In today's society of safe spaces and words that hurt, having some toughness isn't a bad thing. While it's not to say that these things are unimportant, it is impossible to be a fully-functioning and successful adult while relying on someone to designate a safe place. The world is a difficult place. Things don't always happen how we envision them and more often than not, it takes hard work to accomplish what you want to. This is where perseverance comes in. Sports teach us to persevere. They teach us to be tough, to be strong, and to not give up. What else drives the runner on her ten-mile run at practice? What else could drive the baseball player to wake up at four in the morning to practice? What else pushes the wrestler to fight to the very last second to get the win?

Sports help to develop perseverance in a person from a young age and in many ways. Much like some of the other traits, it is developed over time and by many factors. Different types of perseverance show up in youth that play different sports, but all forms translate roughly into the same thing in adulthood. At its root, perseverance is the ability to push through tough times and come back from setbacks to keep working towards a goal. Athletes know this better than anyone. A primary setback that comes with sports is an injury. At some point in their athletic career, the player will experience some sort of injury. The countless hours of stress on the body and dangerous movements that occur make it inevitable. Each sport has its own common injuries, but if one is bad enough, it does the same thing: keep the player from playing. These injuries put athletes into a dark place. Not being able to play, to help your team and teammates, is an extremely helpless and vulnerable feeling. However, like respect, this occurs in a safe environment that allows the individual to learn how to deal with it and become better because of it. As they mature into adulthood, the setback is not usually an injury (although it can be) but some other event that keeps them from doing what they want to. Thanks to his or her experience with youth sports, they know how to handle the setback and keep working to get past it.

Pillar #6: Good Habits

Obesity is currently one of, if not the most, serious health epidemics that face our society today. Unlike the great plagues of days past, this one is something that we not only have a solution for, but a solution that everyone has access to. Exercise and not eating processed junk food all day is the *cure* for obesity. So why is this still a problem? The answer is the lack of good habits and abundance of bad ones that exist for people all over. People choose not to exercise because it's easier not to. They choose to eat junk food instead of healthy food because it tastes better and it, too, is easier. However, it isn't possible to be a good athlete without plenty of exercise and a diet that is nutritious to help replenish the body. This carries over into adult life in the form of good habits. Good habits that have been hammered into a permanent routine over years of participation in sports throughout the formative years.

Adults with a history of participation in youth sports grew up in an environment where physical activity was a part of daily life. In some way, they exercised and got up and moving for a substantial amount of time. Most of the time this was regimented by a coach, but even on off days, athletes tend to find some form of low-intensity exercise; yoga, for example. When they transition out of sports and into adulthood, this daily exercise has often become deeply engrained in their brain and daily routine. This leads to a continuation of that habit in some form. More than likely it is not through sport, but through an alternative exercise. However, regardless of how the exercise is done, it helps to make them healthier and more active.

In another aspect, youth sports help to build strong foundations of good mental habits as well. Players are taught to set their mind to something and then work to accomplish it. The mentality of "if you start something, finish it" is heavily present in sports. Outside of sports, however, its message is equally important. It helps create committed, calm, and responsible individuals. While this is important for professional life, it is even more impactful on the adult social life. Being committed is a rare trait in people today, but it helps to build stronger relationships that are more meaningful and more stable. These good mental habits derived from sports are extremely helpful in adult life.

Pillar #7: Goal Setting

If you've ever wanted to do something and committed to doing it, then you have set a goal for yourself. Nearly everyone has done this. However, the steps you plan to take to reach the goal and the timeframe in which you hope to accomplish it are drastically different for everyone. Sports are a great way to teach goal setting and how to create goals that are SMART. You may have heard of SMART goals before. The word SMART works as an acronym for:

S – Specific

M – Measurable

A – Attainable

R – Realistic

T – Timebound

A SMART goal differs from just a plain goal because it helps define what is needed to reach it and how it will be reached. Whether it is conscious or not, sports provide an excellent way to practice creating and setting these goals over and over. The football player may say, "One day, I want to play in the NFL." Unfortunately, this does not meet the criteria of being a SMART goal. Instead, coaches may help him make a new goal that, while still going in that general direction, is more realistic. He now has the goal of, "When I graduate from high school, I want to have at least three offers to play football in either a D1 or D2 college." This goal is much more specific and realistic for a high school athlete. With hard work and dedication, he can reasonably consider getting multiple college football offers. It is also measurable (at least 3) and time-bound (when I graduate high school). Creating and setting these types of goals is crucial to success later in life. One should constantly be reaching for a goal of some sort. Whether it is getting a promotion, taking a vacation to Hawaii, or finding your soulmate, goals help us to be better versions of ourselves. Youth sports teach us how to make these goals realistically and then chase them down throughout adult life.

From the seven pillars described in detail above, it is plain to see that youth sports offer many significant positive effects later in life. Each of them comes together to form a strong foundation on which to build the rest of one's life, personality, and reputation. Without respect, others will not respect you. Without perseverance, you will not be able to push on through life's hard times. Good habits and goal setting combine to help you lead a healthy adult life and constantly seek to get better. Discipline teaches you to hold fast to your values and keep yourself on track in whatever you are pursuing. Learning structure teaches you to understand the puzzle of the global marketplace and how your job fits into it. Perhaps most importantly, teamwork, a combination of all of these things has taught you that although you are strong, you cannot do it alone. It teaches you that you need the help and cooperation of others to be fully successful. Some may find it hard to believe that shooting hoops in the middle school gym or running around a rubber track can do all of this. Some may wonder how kids and young adult athletes can possess maturity and skill in the many ways they do. Some may only see the final product, a well-rounded adult, and be confused at how they became so well rounded. Youth sports are a fantastic tradition in our society and something that should be not only continued, but encouraged. With more participation in youth sports programs, the next generation of leaders, entrepreneurs, and members of society will be greater than ever and equipped with the tools necessary for success.

About Greg Justice

"Training veteran Greg Justice didn't just get in on the leading edge of an emerging industry, he helped create it. Opening the first personal training studio in Kansas City, Justice has, over the years, laid the groundwork for countless others to follow.

- **Shelby Murphy,** Editor – PFP Magazine, May 2009

Greg Justice, MA, is a best-selling author, speaker and fitness entrepreneur. He opened **AYC Health & Fitness**, Kansas City's Original Personal Training Center, in May 1986. Today, AYC specializes in onsite corporate wellness, personal and small-group training.

Greg is the co-founder and CEO of the **National Corporate Fitness Institute** (NCFI), a certifying body for fitness professionals, and the co-founder of **Scriptor Publishing Group**.

Greg holds a Master's degree in HPER (exercise science) (1986) and a Bachelor's degree in Health & Physical Education (1983) from Morehead State University, Morehead, KY.

He has been actively involved in the fitness industry for more than three decades as a club manager, owner, personal fitness trainer, and corporate wellness supervisor. He has worked with athletes and non-athletes of all ages and physical abilities and served as a conditioning coach at the collegiate level. He worked with the Kansas City Chiefs, during the offseason, in the early 1980's, along with professional baseball, soccer and golf athletes.

Greg has authored 14 books, writes articles and contributes to many publications including, Men's Fitness, Women's Health, Prevention, Time, US News & World Report, New York Times, IDEA Fitness Journal, and Corporate Wellness Magazine. For more information, please visit:

www.GregJustice.com

www.aycfit.com

Chapter 2

Do No Harm

By Debbie Roberts

Owning up

Why did I want to write a chapter in a Sports Performance Book? A couple of things – one is what I experienced and witnessed as a conditioning coach for a local high school. Second, I want to offer coaches, trainers, and parents my 30-years-plus experience in both pre-habilitation and re-habilitation. I have had the privilege of training and treating numerous high school athletes, both amateur and pro athletes in many sports. Two of my specialties are baseball and golf.

I also had the privilege of traveling, training and performing bodywork on a major league baseball player for over 11 years. When he needed some help with the typical aches and pains of playing baseball, I would travel to where he was playing and give him a tune-up. This tune-up consisted of hands-on bodywork, use of multiple tools and techniques, along with resetting the nervous system to help activate muscles to get his body prepared to go out and execute his delivery. I sat behind many home plates and watched his performance, knowing that only hours before he couldn't squat down, he couldn't stand up straight, or his body and muscles were not operating efficiently. I had to think outside the box to keep up with the demands of fixing the race horse right before the race.

We wrote an article together for a national magazine and in the interview, he made the statement that he trusted me because I was never satisfied with what I knew, I was always striving to be better. I couldn't and didn't rely on methods. I used solid principles. Methods are a general law or truth derived from the original principle. If a trainer or coach doesn't have the education or understanding of the basic principles, then it is going to be hard to choose or apply the right method. This is where the client can get hurt or the training doesn't do them any good for their particular sport.

Seeking the understanding of the principles behind the method, in my opinion, really should be the first thought of any trainer or coach.

My career as a trainer and massage therapist has always been seeing training from two sides. The front side is getting the athlete in peak performance shape as a conditioning coach, and the back side is if the athlete suffers an injury.

I had to make sure my education and classes were going to help me understand why an injury would and could occur. This understanding helped me be more effective in both their pre-habilitation and rehabilitation process. I am what you would call an education junkie. When you are trying to help another individual succeed, you have to constantly be asking questions as to *why* something does or doesn't work for them. Gray Cook, the physical therapist who wrote the book, ***Movement***, gave an example of how the central nervous system works differently with each individual. You have two athletes who have injured their ankle, boys, same age, received the same rehabilitation. One gets better and the other one doesn't. Why? Rehabilitation is a central nervous system issue per that individual not per that body part. The body works as a whole, not in picces and parts.

As a solid principle, our approach as trainers, coaches and rehab specialists should be putting the person or individual first, not the method or mode of training. Does your approach hold any carry-over from session to session or to the field?

I attend, at the very least, two major conferences a year to help me be a better movement specialist, then specialty conferences for baseball and golf, along with having the philosophy of learning something new every day. I know that not every injury can be prevented. Some are based on the individual's structure and workout ethics. Coaches and trainers need more education to understand that there are various approaches to doing things safely and effectively without the potential of ruining future careers. One injury can plague the athlete for the rest of their lives.

I know that understanding the principle behind the method is the key. I have treated hundreds of injuries for the past 30-plus years. Many injuries were self-induced because the individual believed in gym know-how versus real science. I have treated many injuries because coaching styles are often antiquated and outdated in their way of thinking and training. The best is when I hear a coach say, "It has always been done this way." Yep, I know but what if we could train more efficiently and effectively, get even better results without the risk and increase in the injury rate?

Risk-to-benefit of the exercise being chosen to perform per that individual should be a solid principle to live by for the future of youth sports. Training groups of players comes with another set of demands on the coach

or trainer. The exercise I can carefully choose for the individual may not work at all for a group.

As I stated earlier, I designed – and helped run for two years in a row – a 29-week pre-conditioning program for a local high school baseball team. It became very clear when we started with their assessments and watched their performance during the program, that the children of today's society are very different than earlier generations. They are more sedentary, they move less, they sit more, they eat more processed foods, and they drink more sports drinks. These children are under more stress, and they have more demands, as the sport-specific training has taken over with the thought processes of parents and coaches that want them to play this one sport year-round. The hope is that by doing these things as a practice, it will guarantee their child will be more successful as a player and would also then lead to having a higher potential of being seen as a future prospect for a college scholarship or pro team. Sadly, nothing is a guarantee, and this is all at the expense of the child's health. To quote the statistics from a *Time* magazine article written and published September 4th, 2017, 483,000 boys play baseball in high school, 1 in 47 will play Division 1, and 1 in 764 will play Major League Baseball.

In this chapter, I would like to offer parents, coaches, personal trainers, chiropractors, physical therapists, and the athletes themselves some insight on how injuries potentially occur during coaching and training. I would also like to offer suggestions on how simple the fix could be by taking on a different viewpoint, and understanding the principles before choosing a method. Within this chapter are some real-life stories that I felt would be of interest to help other trainers and coaches who are facing the same choice. These stories are the proof of how our mindset should change when it comes to training another human being. My passion is helping anyone who is willing to listen to "Stop the Insanity" of poor training and coaching methods.

I believe above all else that the very basic principle behind being a good coach, trainer, or therapist should be putting the client first, along with making choices that have the lowest degree of doing possible permanent harm.

The Perfect Practice

As a coach or medical professional, in order to do no harm, you must start with unyielding principles that will not buy into the garbage that is the latest fad in training. My own training started with great coaches using a good foundation of principles at the early age of five. I swam on a swim team all through grade school, until going to Junior Olympics in high school. The coaches today have too many methods to choose from, are seeking to win at the expense of their players, and preach a constant push, push and push. My coaches had a philosophy that was straightforward, beginning with come and practice the sport over and over again to develop your skill. After the skill has been established, then add *extra* weight training if necessary. Not the reverse thinking of today with train, train, and train so you will be better at your sport. Youth athletes need to develop more skill before adding such large workout loads to their joints and growth plates. A good skill set is what will win the game.

I was fortunate to be coached on good technique during swim practice. Today, private lessons paid for by the parents are the standard way of achieving better techniques, instead of built into the program. These lessons come with a high price tag, and are usually given by an athlete that once played the sport. As a parent, you have to recognize that coaching itself is an art form that requires education and a skill within itself. Not every player who has ever played has the skills or education to be a good coach.

"Practice does not make perfect.
Only perfect practice makes perfect."
-Vince Lombardi

Make Training Count the Right Way

The absolute only way to make training count the right way is to evaluate, assess the athlete, and form a plan from there. In my experience of dealing with parents, coaches, and medical professionals, they encourage kids to participate in a method such as yoga or Pilates for increased flexibility because they think it will be good for them. I am a certified Yoga instructor as well, and I can tell you that I would still need to pick out postures that were appropriate for the child based on their evaluation. Over-stretching is not good for every child if what they really need is more work on their coordination skills or more stability to their joints. I have seen the two extremes in young adolescent males while training them. They are either a Gumby, being way too flexible, or a tin man with not enough tissue extensibility. If you don't assess the child, you are guessing at which training method will ultimately benefit this child the most, and you could have potentially created an increased risk for injury.

A simple principle is to use a functional movement screen and stick to the results of the screen. Strive to help that child become better at their movement pattern.

Running kids seems to be the easiest thing chosen in a coaching tool box to build endurance. First, stop and think; what does that sport really require, less than 30-second bursts of energy more frequently, or 30 minutes of continuous energy? Asking the athlete just to run doesn't improve the athlete overall. It can just produce more problems in the lower extremities. Unless they are going out for long distance running, what are you asking your athlete to do? Baseball, football, basketball, volleyball, tennis, et cetera, all require short bursts of energy of approximately 5 to 20 seconds.

Ask yourself, am I using the right principle before choosing the mode of exercise which is endurance running? Long distance running will have absolutely no carry-over to these sports, because it trains the aerobic energy system, which isn't the energy system being used. In order to improve conditioning, coaches should focus on performing sprints and other explosive movements, with almost full recovery between reps and sets. Performing conditioning work by dragging the sled, pushing the Prowler, battle ropes and running sprints will be more beneficial to players because it will improve work capacity, which is critical to the long-term success of an athlete.

When coaching or training, ask yourself which method or mode of training will produce the most benefits. Will there be carry-over on the field for performance more than the risk of injury in the long haul for this athlete?

One-Food Thought Process Can Do Harm

The coaches asked me to help their players put on some muscle mass. I had our young baseball players do a one-week food diary as part of their conditioning program, and the findings were typical, but startling to me. Some would be considered on the verge of malnutrition, moving towards diabetes, followed by high blood pressure. What I discovered in the process was that the players didn't have a clue about proper nutrition. Most of the players and coaches thought just swigging down a protein shake, eating a lot of chicken and adding in supplements like Creatine or worse would get them bigger. There is a big problem with the one-food thought process. Like all other aspects of training, the athlete's nutritional needs should be calculated per that individual. The diet for repair and growth should have a decent balance of proteins, carbohydrates, fats, sodium, water, with no foods that contain additives. Nutrition is really too broad a subject for one chapter, but I wanted to discuss what I saw and heard which was alarming to me in our adolescents.

Supplements, like protein drinks, are to supplement a good diet, not make up for a poor diet. They are supposed to supplement something you are not getting in your diet. There should be a need for a supplement. An over-abundance of supplements in the human system can do harm or just the opposite – go straight down the toilet. The kids are looking for something easy, instead of learning how to shop, cook or make better choices. What I experienced with the parents, coaches and players was a real need to go back to the basics of being prepared, cooking, and not relying so heavily on convenience foods.

Bottom line, no matter what mode of training you give the kids, if they don't eat, they will get skinny, not bigger.

Creatine has gotten a lot of press with the bodybuilding world and has trickled down into the high schools. Teaching our young athletes where the source of a supplement comes from is critical to help them understand that they don't actually need the supplement. Wild game is the richest dietary source of Creatine, according to the University of Maryland Medical Center. Game meats include rabbit, venison, elk, wild boar, ostrich, moose, buffalo, bison, squab and wild duck. Creatine is also found in domestic meat. Free-range meats are likely to offer a richer source of Creatine than commercially produced meats. Lean meat options include chicken breast, turkey breast, Cornish hen, lamb chops and veal loin. Most of America can get their fill of Creatine by EATING. It may be hard if you are vegetarian to get an extra load of Creatine, but unless you are an endurance athlete or your body weight matters to your sport, your need to supplement may not be necessary, anyway. Baseball and golf are not endurance sports and do not necessarily require a large body mass to be successful.

The Perfect Storm

Do you know what happens with the combination of too much protein and too much Creatine supplement? This combination can become an additional stress on the kidneys. One of my high-level ball players will tell you it can certainly earn you a trip to the emergency room. He passed out while training and had to been taken to the hospital and given fluids to bring him back in balance. In one of my training sessions during a routine leg work out, I had a guy get faint and end up on the floor. I asked him what he had done that day. He admitted to supplementing with Creatine. This can make a perfect storm of fluid imbalances. If you add in the typical athlete's fast food, high-sodium diet, not enough water per that individual, plus Creatine as a supplement, you create an imbalance in the body's electrolyte system which helps move that individual towards kidney failure. My girlfriend, while working as a nurse practitioner, witnessed this on several occasions in her office.

These were just kids making a ton of nutritional mistakes using fast foods, supplementing with protein shakes, some were flirting with taking Creatine and some just not eating anything that resembled balance. Sodium seemed to be a real issue. According to the dietary guidelines for Americans, it is recommended that Americans consume less than 2,300 milligrams (mg) of sodium per day as part of a healthy eating pattern. Based on these guidelines, the vast majority of adults eat more sodium than they should—an average of more than 3,400 mg each day. Eating too much sodium puts Americans at risk for developing serious medical conditions, like high blood pressure, heart disease, and stroke.

Teenage boys are some of the worst offenders of high-sodium diets. According to the health.gov dietary guidelines, male teens between the ages of 12 to 19 consume, on the average, about 4,300 milligrams of daily sodium. Teen girls in this age group get about 2,900 milligrams, which is still more than the recommendation. When you have too much sodium in your diet, fluid balance suffers. Your system holds on to an abnormally large amount of water and your heart has to pump harder to get blood through your system. Not only does your blood pressure go up, but so does your risk of developing heart disease. Changing our young athletes' eating habits at an early age helps set them up for success, so they are less likely to suffer from chronic conditions as adults.

Antiquated Coaching

To help reinforce what improper coaching and this electrolyte imbalance can contribute to, I will relay the story of a mother who is also a friend of mine. It was Hell Week, where they try to make the kids tough by running them to death and telling them they are weak if they need water. Her son told her earlier in the week, "Mom, I think I am going to die." Then she got the dreaded call in the middle of the night that her son was in extreme back pain and couldn't get up out of bed. He felt terrible and had chills since that day's training which was, in his words, "Brutal." Because of his personal dietary choices of protein drinks, not enough water, combined with the Hell Week practice of this particular college coaching staff, he was going into kidney failure. She told him to call 911 and get to the hospital. Because of that phone call he did survive, but barely. He had to spend a week in the hospital and have I.V. fluids to get back in balance.

Let's stop and think again for one minute about our athletes. They are not machines, but human beings. You can't just change the oil and hope they keep going. None of this way of thinking is a solid nutritional goal for athletes, especially the young ones whose systems are fragile, anyway.

During the baseball preconditioning, we educated the players on the importance of weighing themselves before coming to the field. If they had lost two pounds from the morning weigh-in, this was a way for them to see that they might in fact be dehydrated. We tried to instill in them that they needed to have fluids and replace those two pounds before coming to the field.

An easy principle to teach would be you can't get big muscles by eating or drinking processed foods. You cannot make a stronger player or team without addressing their nutritional habits. Teach them, if it comes in a bottle (unless it is water), bag or can, it has been altered by man, and offers less muscle-building qualities. This usually gets their attention!

Knowledge is Necessary for Coaching Athletics

Being asked to write a preconditioning program for a local high school, I found out that many school budgets don't have any money allocated for an athletic trainer to run a preconditioning or conditioning program for sports. So, coaches might have to resort to telling the young athlete to join a gym. Okay, sounds like a plan, but with little-to-no knowledge from the coach on the specifics of what a conditioning program in a gym should look like, the kids are left to their own devices. The need for education on writing a proper sports-specific conditioning program by the coach or parent is something that is rarely addressed. Most young athletes need to work on coordination and skills first, not muscle building in a gym.

Children have growth plates to be considered and not all children's growth plates close at the same rate of time. Boys' growth plates close between the ages of 15 to 17, and girls a little earlier, between the ages of 12-15, which means that there is always a possibility of too much stress from practice, playing or working out being put on the bones or joints. These children can develop stress fractures, or worse.

Here is another crazy story of defective coaching. A very frustrated mother brought her son in for an evaluation. He was nine. His chief complaint was that he couldn't run. He had been seen by an orthopedic physician and a chiropractor who had no answers for her. She had filmed him running, and she could see something was wrong. She was upset because the coach just kept yelling at her son to run faster, when clearly he couldn't. The coach suggested personal training to make him stronger, but that didn't work, either.

Ready for what I saw during the movement screen? Just standing in front of me, his foot was rotated out to the side at a 45-degree angle. When he squatted down, the foot continued to rotate out even further. When asked directly, he had landed on the side of his foot while playing on a trampoline a few months earlier. After the initial pain, he didn't complain, so the mother thought it was healed. This injury wasn't assessed or addressed before he started playing baseball in his season.

I recommended she take him to a sports podiatrist. One x-ray later, this child had been trying to run on nine stress fractures in his foot. The child had no real foot pain, but again pointed to the outside of his ankle when asked directly.

Let me ask you, could you run if your foot was sitting sideways or had nine fractures?

The principle to learn would be to look, ask, and really listen to the player before having them start any conditioning program. Let them know that it is okay and you are here to help them become better. As the coach, go to classes and learn how to do a functional movement screen or find a trainer that can do these evaluations for your team to rule out potential injuries or obvious joint misalignments that need to be addressed before the season starts.

Don't assume the child is uncoordinated or lazy. There is an emotional pain of being constantly yelled at by a coach to do something that maybe they can't physically do. I will refer you to Dr. Andrew's book that is titled, ***Any Given Monday***, where he, too, addresses the need to ask the child direct questions and then really listen.

Pain is Real

In my experience, I have seen both parents and coaches encouraging players to play even when they are sore or in some degree of pain. Standard advice to the child from either party is ice whatever is sore, take some Advil, and you will be all right tomorrow. I believe too many coaches and parents think the child is trying to get out of something, rather than something is really wrong. The incredible pressure put on a child to play through pain is absurd. To quote a common statement, "Well, he or she acted like it wasn't that bad."

STOP THE INSANITY NOW! All pain is a warning sign that something is out of balance. Taking over-the-counter pain relievers should not be a full-time practice. Not all pain should be drowned out. It is a signal, a message to the brain that this child either needs rest or help with recuperation. Coaches, trainers and parents – stop and take the time to really listen, ask questions directly. Something is either not right or beginning to become a problem.

I don't mean to be harsh, but can we please all take a step back from needing to win or play all the time, and remember there is a child involved, not a wind-up toy or android. These are not little robots that are invincible.

The kids confide in me that they don't want the coaches to know they are hurt, because maybe they won't let them be on the team. They don't want the parents to know because they are afraid they won't let them play. In addition, the kids feel like nobody is listening to them, anyway. One child I treated had a severe tendonitis caused by an internal rotation of the humerus, which was diagnosed by MRI. He was still expected to show up to practice and play in the game because the coach needed him. Yikes!

A father brought his son into my office complaining of shoulder pain and weakness. His father wanted him to have a massage treatment with me. However, after the screen, I declined to give him the massage. The screen revealed a possible labral tear.

The father said to me, "Can't you just give him a massage to help with the pain? He only has to finish the year out and there are going to be scouts at this next outing." I told the father that it would not be in the best interest of the child if I treated him. I explained to him that I could relieve the symptoms just enough that his son could play and do even further damage to the shoulder. My recommendation would be to go get an orthopedic exam. The mother called me one week later and thanked me. An MRI had revealed the boy had a second significant tear which needed to be repaired. Luckily, the doctor told them if he did the surgery now, he would be able to play for his scholarship next year, and he did.

If we stop to consider, where is the principle in this way of thinking when it comes to children? I know playing is important, I know winning is important, but isn't the child's future important? Pain is real. It is a real signal. Please don't ignore it. These kids' voices need to be heard.

Methods Versus Principles

As a trainer, coach, or parent, you are exposed to hundreds, if not thousands, of methods these days. Which one do you choose, when they all claim to give great results? CrossFit is a great training method, but for only a certain amount of the population, because it requires an incredible amount of joint alignment and stability to do those Olympic lifts.

Sadly, one of the stories is about a young boy trying to get ready for baseball season. He went to one of these programs very deconditioned, thinking he would get in condition. He tried too hard to keep up with the adults in the class, and consequently, sustained an injury of a non-union fracture to his back. He was out for the season and may never be able to play again. Yes, this unfortunately is a true story. No one wants to believe that a devastating injury can happen that fast. In a one-hour workout, this child's life was changed forever.

This is why I am obsessed with helping coaches and trainers understand principles before choosing their methods.

I want to give credit where it should be given from a book written by Evan Osars, titled ***Corrective Exercise Solutions*** *to Common Hip and Shoulder Dysfunction.* In his book he addresses the need for having a principle way of thinking, instead of method way of thinking. As I was reading this book, it hit me, I had always questioned methods. If it didn't make sense or have a scientific reason somewhere behind it, I just wasn't quick to get on board and add it to my training tool box.

Raise Them Up

Our young people are the prospects of the future. I find one of the most rewarding moments as a trainer is when you get to cultivate young people into good athletes with good principles. They are our future prospects of either our college programs or for a few of them, the possibility of a major league career.

Being a female trainer in a man's world, particularly baseball, I have seen and heard it all. The following statements are the ones that made me question and say, "Hmm?" Listen with me and evaluate the coaching style. I would like you to consider enough is enough with this way of thinking.

The coach states, "I want to weed them out."

Coaches and trainers, the things to consider are whether you are being objective or subjective. Are you weeding out the ones you subjectively don't like or the ones who need your help with developing their skill set? Don't forget, children do grow up with help.

The coach states, "I only want the ones that have the greatest mental fortitude on my team."

Coaches and trainers – the things to consider are that they are not 25 years of age yet. Mental fortitude is developed over time, sometimes years beyond what you might think. That is what coaching is about, developing mental and physical skills.

The coach states, "Let's work them hard today because they were lazy at practice last night."

Coaches and trainers – the thing to consider is whether they were lazy, or did you not connect with them in the right way? Or, was their nutrition so poor they had no fuel? Are you being objective or are you subjectively putting your day and problems on them?

The coach states, "He's faking it, he wants attention. He isn't really hurt." Coaches, trainers, and parents, I can tell you that there are probably a few who can fake it, but orthopedic evaluations and questions are something the child has never heard. So, hold that judgment call until all evidence points that way. Here is an example. A child comes to me complaining of shoulder pain during the conditioning. I had observed him not being able to do certain tasks. When I did the Manual Muscle testing to his rotator cuff, I found his infraspinatus, one of the posterior shoulder muscles, to be weak. I talked with the coach. His statement was, "He is lazy and is probably faking it."

I suggested an orthopedic exam. After a doctor's examination and MRI, he was suffering with a severe tendonitis. This kid was not being viewed fairly based on his physical appearance of being overweight. Things to consider – are you being understanding or subjectively judgmental?

The coach states, "He doesn't have what it takes to get the job done."

Coaches and trainers – the thing to consider would be that the child in this case was only 14. Testosterone levels change as our children grow and age, which makes them stronger. Consider giving children time to develop and grow into themselves.

The coach states, "I need number ones on my team to win."

Coaches and trainers – I don't deny you need some number ones to win a game. But isn't it our duty as trainers and coaches to help coach those number twos and threes into ones, let alone the fours and fives?

Coaching is a big undertaking and responsibility. Find ways to be objective while producing number ones. This is not only your future, but theirs as well.

Here is a principle to consider. I don't think we need more methods of training, I think when it comes to sports performance, we need better clarity on the way to think while we are training.

To the Coach

I do understand that to be considered the best coach, you must breed winners. You have to demand respect and preach honor and integrity. Your philosophy affects each player and the team as a whole. It's no easy checklist. Strive to find the balance between winning and player development.

And to the Player

I wish I could tell you there is a particular secret that no one has let out, but the truth is there are several factors that can, but don't always, lead to becoming a pro athlete. Either way, though, they will always make you better.

1. **Hard work** – Hard work means doing *more* than anyone ever expects you to do. Do you have an inner passion that makes you work that hard? Can you train and maintain yourself without being coached to do so?

2. **Dedication** – I don't and won't miss an opportunity to do **1%** better every day, the Todd Durkin philosophy. Dedication isn't about dedication to your workout program, your Mom or Dad. Dedication is a spirit within to practice whatever it is to be better than yesterday. Our cells die and regenerate daily, that means that there is always a new you when you wake up. Use that to your advantage!

3. **Drive** – You must have an inner desire to hold your dreams, your goals, and your desires to the highest standards. You uplift your own spirit and look for more ways to do everything better without being told.

4. **Principles** – Always look for the principle behind the method. Your principles become who you are and how you develop.

It has been a privilege to offer you this information. The heart of athletes and our youth depend on it.

Happy coaching!

About Debbie Roberts

Debbie Roberts, LMT is the innovator of the *Assessment, Treatment & Muscle Stabilization (ATM) System*. She is an international author and speaker, founder of *Debbie Roberts Seminars*, a CEU program providing continuing education for massage therapists and personal trainers. Certified through the National Academy of Sports Medicine, NCBTMB, TPI Medical Level 3, and the Florida Board of Massage, Debbie is best known for her unparalleled understanding of the anatomy of an injury and her focus on assessment and treatment plans. Debbie is a multi-year presenter for the Florida State Massage Therapy Association, American Massage Association, Club and Fitness Association, and the Florida Chiropractic Association.

Visit www.debbierobertsseminars.com for more information.

Chapter 3

Bang! Pop!
Why Sports Performance?

by Nathan Yamnitz

Sports have been incredibly important to me for my entire life. At the age of one, right after I learned to walk, my mom went out and got me a whiffle ball bat, a glove, a ball, and a tee, so I could learn how play baseball. My dad went and got me a little Fisher Price hoop and a ball, so I could learn to play basketball. I never stopped after that point. For hours and hours and hours a day, all I wanted to do was play.

I grew up with a sister with severe special needs. Kristen was just under two years younger than me and was born with a brain disease called Lissencephaly. That meant that while she would physically grow, her brain would stay that of an infant for the duration of her life. She wasn't supposed to live past the age of two. Kristen ended up making it to the age of 18 because of the tremendous amount of love and care that my parents, our family and friends would give to her. However, it definitely led to a lot of tough times for me.

I'm not complaining. I love my sister and every single thing about the relationship that I had, and still to this day continue to have with her even though she's gone. Knowing, caring for, and loving my sister during my formative years laid the foundation for becoming the man that I am today. I feel her presence with me during the daily decisions that I make. And, many of the things that I do are a direct result of the simple fact that she couldn't do those things. She has been my best friend, my greatest teacher, and my inspiration. But as a kid, one has to deal with his friends and classmates making fun of him or his family because he has a sister who is "mentally retarded." (Sidenote: Any of my athletes that I train right now will tell you that that word still bothers me. You can get away with saying just about anything you want in the gym, but the use of the 'R' word is sure to land you 10 burpees.) I was seen as different from the rest of my peers, through no fault of my own, and I didn't understand it. The one thing I could do was compete on the field or on the court. There, I was equal. There, nothing else mattered. So that's what I poured myself into, playing sports with everything I had. It was my escape and my greatest comfort during the trying times of childhood.

If I had the choice, I would have played sports my entire life, competitively or recreationally. It was all I wanted to do. And then one day, I couldn't anymore. My body wouldn't let me. I was a senior in high school, 17 years old, when I took a service trip to Belize City with six of my fellow classmates from my school, De Smet Jesuit in Saint Louis. We went down there to teach in St. Martin De Porres School, one of the poorest schools, in one of the poorest and most crime-ridden areas of Belize City. Before school each day, we would play basketball with the kids, and after school, we would play soccer. It was Belize versus the United States, 32 of them against seven of us. The joy that sports brought to them was incredible to behold.

"Dunk the ball, Mr. Nathan! Dunk the ball!"

"Will you guys play soccer with us after school?"

"Of course we will."

I couldn't want anything more. It was during the middle of one of those afternoon soccer games that everything changed. We were about an hour and a half into our second game of the week. It was 90 degrees and humid. We were hot, sweaty, and elated to be on the field. The score was 2-2 and time was running out. We would have to head back to the host family soon, so it was now or never if we were going to score. I positioned myself at the top of the box and received a cross off my chest. I spun to launch the ball toward the goal. This would be it! And in an instant, it wasn't. BANG! POP! And I crumbled to the ground in pain, yelling out, "Aaahhh!" A moment later I heard a voice about five feet to my left say, "Are you okay? Did it get you?"

"Did what get me?" I responded. "That was my knee."

"They shot you in the knee?" the Belizean boy asked.

"Shot me? No! That *was* my knee!"

And then I looked up and saw three boys around me, lying on the ground with their hands covering their heads. Drive-by shootings and violence were such a common thing in this area, and the sound of my knee imploding upon itself was so loud that these kids thought that I had been shot.

After returning home and having surgery, I faced a long rehabilitation process. Six to seven months, and hours upon hours of stretching and strengthening soft tissue work, stem treatment and ice baths, and my knee still wasn't feeling perfect, but I had the doctor's okay to start playing sports. Two weeks later, and I was on the ground in pain again.

"Seriously? You have got to be kidding," I thought. I just spent six months, and I don't know how many hundreds of hours rehabbing this thing, and here I am again? I couldn't believe it, yet there I was, six more months before I was back to full strength. But I wasn't really back to full strength. Sure, there were times when everything worked just fine. Times when I could take off knowing that everything was going to work, and soar through the air to dunk a basketball, one of the greatest feelings in the world. Then there were other times when for no apparent reason, my leg just wouldn't fire. I would drive the lane to elevate, only to feel like I was actually jumping down in the end. And the pain; the pain and discomfort had never gone away.

Fast forward two to three more years, and as a 21-year-old, I am now realizing that this is probably going to be me for the rest of my life – a dysfunctional knee that still experiences stabbing pain. It was also during this time that we lost my sister, my first memory, my oldest friend. All of the pain of childhood seemed to rush back into my life, and this time I didn't have the outlet of playing sports to comfort me, to take my mind off of things. I was defeated in just about every way.

I had been training people for about three years at this point and had taken on a new job at a reputable training facility in the area. It was there that I met one of my first mentors. Jim Adams was a massive individual, with a huge chest, shoulders, and biceps, and an even bigger smile and personality. He was intimidating yet inviting, and I had to interview with him before I could get the job. So, I did what any ambitious person would do before interviewing with somebody; I looked him up on the internet. What I found was a long list of certifications and degrees just like any other trainer has, but then something stuck out to me. Underneath the "Why I Train" portion of Jim's profile, it read, "My main goal is to improve my client's ability to move. If I can improve their ability to move, I have improved their life." I immediately decided to adopt this axiom as my own. To this day, I'm not sure that Jim knows just how much he did for a young 21-year-old trainer trying to make his way in the industry. I will always be incredibly grateful for all the help and support that he provided me. Thanks, Jim!

So, I had my new charge, my new goal – figure out how to help people learn to move better! Better movement, not just more movement would be the key. Progression would not be measured by the total weight moved or the amount of repetitions completed, but by the quality and difficulty of the movement being performed. After some digging and rooting around, I finally landed upon Gray Cook and the Functional Movement Screen. Gray is a physical therapist by trade, and a master of movement correction. Watching his videos and how he changed movement patterns with ease, always leading to a more functional person, amazed me. This is what I needed to learn – but there was more! Gray subscribed to the theory of the joint-by-joint approach. In his mind, the body was just a stack of joints, or a series of joints, each with its own specific function. If there was a problem with an athlete's ankles, you wouldn't always see it there. Sometimes you would see it one joint higher up the chain, at the knee. Suddenly everything made sense.

Nearly two decades of playing basketball and constantly rolling and spraining my ankles had left them fairly dysfunctional. My body didn't have anywhere else to get the mobility required for my ankles, except from my knee, which is a joint designed to be stable. I started thinking that maybe the 14 months that I had spent rehabbing not one, but two knee injuries had been nearly a complete waste of time, because I had not addressed my ankle. This was big. This was next-level-big, in my opinion. Why hadn't anyone ever taught me this before? There was a problem with our system. There was a problem with the way that we trained youth athletes, and it still exists predominantly today, though many top trainers, coaches, and therapists are making it their mission to bridge this gap in knowledge and understanding of how the body works.

I put myself back into the rehabilitation process, but this time, I was auditing the class online. I was studying the functional movement screen and learning the proper correctives. I was using Google, YouTube, and anything else I could find to learn how to fix my body. But I wasn't worried about knees. I was worried about my ankles. It has now been nearly a decade since this revelation, and while my legs still do not fire perfectly at all times, I haven't had pain in at least seven years. I have been able to get back out onto the basketball court, the soccer field, and a baseball field. I've been able to play football with my friends, and to feel the joy of being a kid again. Not only that, but I found my new calling – to give athletes the best training that they can possibly get without compromising anything. We will keep our athletes on the field. We will protect. We will correct. We will perform.

When I got first into work as a personal trainer or a strength coach after that devastating knee injury at the end of my high school career, I had always written up my own workouts and developed my own vertical jump programs, which people were interested in because there weren't that many 5'10" or 5'11" white guys who could throw one down off the backboard. After a couple of years of mixed results, I began to get discouraged. It was hard to train athletes all year round. At this point, many people believed it was still more intelligent to stop weight lifting during the season in all sports but football. I would have times that were very busy, and times that were not busy at all based on what sports my athletes were playing.

I began to slip more into the realm of general fitness, but always kept that athletic edge in mind with how I trained my clients. And about four years ago, at the time of writing this, I was blessed to be introduced to a young man who would change my life forever. The hours that I spent with Jack that first summer that I trained him, as an eighth grader who excelled at soccer, basketball, and baseball, filled me up with a passion and energy that I had not experienced in years. I knew then that this is what I wanted to do. I wanted to train athletes. And through my work with this young man, many others started to follow. And then as Malcolm Gladwell would say, I reached a tipping point about two years later.

I didn't have to tip-toe around anymore, acting like I was the guy who would train anyone and everyone. I am the guy who trains athletes. And I train them to be safe, high-performing individuals. As I remind them frequently and every good coach knows, availability trumps ability any day of the week. You could be the most talented athlete on the face of the planet, but if you spend 80% of your season on the bench because of injury, you're no good to that coach. I have spent the last decade of my life dedicating myself to learning from the greatest minds in the performance training world and am fully aware that these are the giants on whose shoulders I stand today, like Todd Durkin, Mike Boyle, and Charles Poliquin. The wealth of information available today is at an all- time high. And I have charged myself with the responsibility of synthesizing the ideas of these great minds.

How can I bring everything together, add in my own flavor and beliefs, and present the best program possible to the world? It's not easy, I will tell you that, especially in the "results now" world that we live in today. Athletic performance is at an all-time high, and the injuries are escalating with it. I have been fortunate enough to work with some pretty spectacular athletes, some who you know and some who you will know very soon. And the one thing they all have in common is that they don't take shortcuts. The best of the best don't just spend time developing their skills for years and years and years. They spend time sharpening their minds, developing their athleticism, and bullet-proofing their bodies. This may mean that they won't see a huge increase in their personal bests in the weight room right away. Their velocity on the mound, or their vertical jump, or their sprinting speed may not immediately increase, but if they are doing things the right way, they will be better for it. Those results will come, and injuries will not.

Growing up with a loved one who could not perform the day-to-day movement tasks required by most, and going through my own injuries, has filled me with a passion for human movement. The ability to learn how to move better and how to stay on the field or on your feet is one of the most precious gifts that we can be given. Do not take this for granted. Find coaches who believe the same. Assess. Protect. Correct. Perform. Follow that simple recipe to stay healthy and in the game. Then, most importantly, hold on to the joy that movement brings. The feel of the ball hitting the bat or glove, the grass between your toes, the taste of sweat dripping off your lips, and the pure bliss that comes from moving perfectly through space. Should you ever need guidance in your quest for premium human performance, please don't hesitate to reach out to myself or any of the other coaches at The Performance Zone. It is more than just a place. It is a higher state of mind. For an athlete, there is no better place to be than *in the zone*; completely connected in mind, body, and spirit. That is what we do. And that is our wish for you!

About Nathan Yamnitz

Nathan Yamnitz is the Founder, CEO, and Head Trainer of Performance Zone Fitness. Growing up playing every sport he could find, Nathan gravitated toward baseball and basketball the most. After multiple injuries ended his athletic endeavors, he began working as a personal trainer. He trained for other companies for a few years, then decided to branch out on his own in the general health and fitness training industry in 2011. In 2016, he founded The Performance Zone, an elite human performance training center that specializes in movement improvement and athletic performance.

If he's not in the gym, he's either playing golf, hanging out with his dogs, traveling, or learning something new. (The pursuit of knowledge is never to be completed and is often undervalued.) If you ever have any questions or interest that you think Nathan or the other trainers at The Performance Zone could address, please do not hesitate to reach out!

Chapter 4

In-STILLed

By Art Still

"We are not a Team because we work together. We are a Team because we trust, respect and care for each other."

– Vala Afshar

I grew up being part of a team. My head coaches were my parents, James and Gwendolyn. My teammates were Sparky, Bonnie, Francine, Francina, Wendell, Gary, Dennis, Valerie, Jacqueline and then, of course, there was yours truly. Our mother was, without a doubt, the captain of our team. She was really the head of the family – the matriarch in our tribe.

What she instilled in us (Get it? In-STILLed?) was anchored in the value of relationships. She created a culture in our 'team' amongst all the negative and imperfect players. One thing that always stood out to me was the fact that my mother recognized her limitations and encouraged us to weed out the negative and to focus on the positive, even taking it to the next level. That was the foundation our team was built on. It has continued to be part of my game plan into my adult life, within my family, school, community, sports, and business.

My mother gave birth to ten kids in 13 years. I was number six in line, the fifth birth. I have twin sisters older than me. There were four of us boys born within a five-year span – Wendell, myself, Gary and Dennis. I believe this is where working as a team began. My mother had a game plan in place and teaching us to be responsible and accountable was the most important part of that plan. She had chores for us to accomplish, like making our beds and such, but what I remember the most was that every Saturday she would wax the floors. She would give us boys old blankets folded, and we would slide across the floors pretending like we were driving cars. For us, it was fun and for my mother, she accomplished the task she set out to do, shining her floors. If we chose not to complete our chores or didn't do them up to par, there would be a consequence. Most of the time, if we got in trouble it was always ALL of us. With what little we had, we were taught great lessons of value.

So what are some of these values that have made me who I am today (please don't ask members of my original team) that have been an important ingredient and given me a positive purpose in LIFE? And how have these positive values helped me, not only in sports but ultimately in the Big Game: "LIFE?"

For starters, we learned how important it is to work together as a team. At a young age, we never had vacations or traveled. We grew up in the projects in Camden, New Jersey. Our recreation was sports, not organized. We didn't have much grass, but what was there we utilized and made our own football field. My brothers, Wendell, Gary and Dennis would play on the half asphalt, half grass field, using an old Quaker Oats box as a football. Generally, it was Dennis and myself on one team, like defensive linesman because we were bigger, against Gary and Wendell, offensive players because they were smaller and faster. Nine times out of ten the game would end when we would start fighting and our 'football' was deflated – the original Deflate-Gate.

We also played with others in our neighborhood, which widened out our team. Some of the guys like Butch, Kenny, Peaches, Carlos, Joel, Lloyd and Robert were always part of the team, whether we were playing stickball, basketball, football, rolling tires or chasing tomato trucks. We shared a common bond in life and those relationships help solidify my character. We also knew that our mothers were a team in the sense that they all looked out for the interests of all of us kids in the projects. They had a common bond and goal of helping all the children to become responsible adults.

Another value that was instilled in me at a young age was that of perseverance and structure. I never thought too much about it until I became an adult, but my mother taught us the importance of perseverance. She was, by far, the most spiritual person I knew. Although I didn't understand it as a child, I am thankful for it now. Two times a week, she would dress up all ten of us kids and walk over two miles to and from the Broadway Baptist Tabernacle for Bible study and prayer meetings. She did this in the rain, shine, snow and heat. She valued the importance of teaching us that we are accountable to our Creator for the way we live our lives, the choices we make and the way we treat others, regardless of skin color or nationality. Her example of perseverance and consistency was solidly intertwined in my sports performance.

Many of the people that attended the Broadway Baptist Tabernacle were like extended family members. The Warrens, Roziers, Drummonds, Gilberts and Sister Ruth were some of the people who created this team. Brother Dawson was one of my biggest influencers at a young age. He used to be a heavyweight boxer. His whole life centered around doing the right thing in every aspect of his life – how you eat, exercise, help others, discipline, structure and so on. He took all of the young ones, especially the boys, and talked to us about the value of doing what was right and goal setting. There were times when he would take me and my other three brothers to his home in the country where we would help him work outside. He would provide instructions and then work side by side with us. He set a fine example teaching us what a man is and how to be a positive leader. He didn't just speak words, he lived them.

Interestingly, the Rozier family attended the church and my mother and Bea Rozier became good friends. They had a common bond. Bea was raising a number of boys, and she and my mother stood by the same principles and were the closest of friends. One of Bea's sons, Mike, went to one of our rival schools in Camden, Woodrow Wilson High School. Mike later went on to receive the Heisman Trophy in 1983 and was drafted in 1984 to the Houston Oilers, first-round, second player picked.

Coincidentally, go back five years to 1978, and there was another young one that attended the Broadway Baptist Tabernacle who was also drafted first-round, second player picked to the Kansas City Chiefs. Guess who? Yours, truly!

Because of the age difference, we never played against each other on the high school or college level. The first time we played against each other was in the NFL. If you ask

Mike today about his mother and lessons learned in his early childhood, he will tell you his mother and my mother might as well have been twins.

The value of respect should not be underestimated when it comes to sports. In the late '60s and '70s, serious racial issues were prevalent. One of the big issues we faced was that we were from the inner city, and we played schools from the suburbs. These schools had an economic advantage in every aspect. On top of that, Camden High's arch rival was a parochial school, Bishop Eustace. They, too, had an economic advantage being a private school. With all the tension surrounding us, our coach, Andy Hinson and his staff kept us focused on what was important, teaching us life skills and respect in these troublesome times while playing our sport. He wanted us to be student athletes. Bishop Eustace was highly competitive and always the top of the conference and state in all sports. This is where Rick Fromm and Jim Ryan come into the picture. Both Rick and Jim went to Bishop Eustace. We had the privilege of playing against each other. I did not know either of them personally. What I did know was that when it came to playing the game, we were about the 'big win' and to prove to these rich white kids that it wasn't about money, houses, cars or education. It was about your heart.

As a matter of fact, my senior year in 1973, our record in football was 8-0-1. The one tie was against Bishop Eustace and the score was 0-0. After my senior year, I was privileged to get a full scholarship to the University of Kentucky. That is where Rick, my "Brother from another Mother," and I were reunited as teammates playing the same position, different sides. He was there a couple of years before me, and when I arrived, he took me under his wing and helped me transition into that environment. Here is where respect comes into play. If I was taught to have a serious dislike for opposing players, it would've presented a major problem when I found myself on the same team. Instead, respect for the game and Rick gave me the honor of having a life-long friendship. I'd like to add that I got to know Rick's green '72 Nova really well riding back and forth from Lexington, Kentucky to Camden, New Jersey, a 12-hour drive back then. It helped me to get home to see my other "team mates."

As for Jim Ryan, we played against each other in the NFL for ten years, 20 games. He played with the Denver Broncos at the same time I played with the Kansas City Chiefs, another rival team. Jim had a very successful career in the NFL as a player, and currently, Jim is coaching with the Houston Texans.

Many of the values I learned such as respect, perseverance, discipline, teamwork, and structure were taught to me at a young age and rolled over into my youth and early adulthood. I feel that although I had already applied many of these values in my life, they were only enhanced and refined throughout my college days and beyond. I would be remiss not to acknowledge that those who have taught me these values were committed to them as well. Coach Vince Lombardi once said, "Individual commitment to a group effort – that is what makes a team work, a company work, a society work, a civilization work."

Throughout my high school, college, and NFL careers, I was fortunate enough to have multiple excellent head coaches and assistant coaches that were part of the group effort. Coach Andy Hinson was my coach at Camden High School, and he had a great impact on my life. He was a father figure for me. He knew I had the athletic ability to earn a scholarship in either basketball or football. When making the decision, he had me reason on which sport would be to my advantage. I was about 6'7" and weighed about 190 pounds. Coach Hinson had me visualize where the best opportunity for me would be, where I'd be able to play and make a name for myself. With that reasoning and making an informed decision, I eventually went to the University of Kentucky (the highest academic university on this side of the Mississippi River), because they were rebuilding their program and were looking to build a championship team.

What Coach Hinson said to me became a reality. At UK, Coach Fran Curci built a winning team. In my junior year, we were 9-3 and won our conference. We played in, and won, the Peach Bowl. Also, in those two years, Penn State was the football powerhouse in the country. The only loss they had in two seasons was against University of Kentucky on their field and at home the following year. In my senior year, we were 10-1 and ranked 6th in the country. Coach Curci is what I would call a true general. He had assistant coaches who went on to become head coaches at other schools.

Another influencer who encouraged discipline, respect, and other values was Pat Etcheberry. He was my strength and conditioning coach in college. He was a very important role model back then and continues to be a good friend and role model today. To this day, he is still actively training elite and professional athletes in a number of countries. He still has the tenacity he had back in my college days, along with the onion breath (he is all about eating nutritious whole foods). On to the next phase, the NFL.

In 1978, I was fortunate to be drafted by the Kansas City Chiefs in the first round, second player picked behind Earl Campbell, the Heisman Trophy Winner, and a person who can cause some serious headaches for you when you try to tackle him. To be honest with you, when I was growing up, my brothers were big KC Chiefs fans – me, a Raider. I can remember all of the battles between them. But once I got drafted by the Chiefs, I was forever a Chief. I can recall before games some of the big players like Bobby Bell, Buck Buchannan, Curtis McClinton, Lenny Dawson, Ed Budde, Ed Lothamer and others would walk through the locker room. I viewed it as a privilege to be able to see and talk to them. Now we are all lifelong friends, part of a brotherhood. And I couldn't forget Lamar Hunt. He wasn't just the owner of the organization, he was a great person.

During my first spring training with the Kansas City Chiefs in May of 1978, I started developing relationships with many of the players on the team. This included draftees, rookies, free agents and veterans. One person that I had a special bond with that continues on through today is Walter White. He took me under his wing. I can remember the first day of practice, the KC Royals were playing. We went to the game and hung out. Walter White is also one of the founders of the Kansas City Ambassadors which I am a part of today. There are over 35 retired players involved with the Ambassadors. Some of them I played ball with, some are older and some are younger. The Kansas City Ambassadors is a tight-knit group and have become recognizable throughout the NFL, serving as an innovative and worthy asset to the Chiefs Community Caring Team in the Kansas City region and beyond. The Ambassadors are the only group of their kind in the NFL and inductees into the group are hand-picked based on tenure and their willingness to participate in Ambassador outreach events and meetings. We support our community with local scholarship programs, charity golf tournaments and numerous charitable visits and appearances.

As any fan knows, there is a very strong dislike in football between the offense and the defense. There is also another dislike. When rookies come in, there are sometimes conflicts as positions are threatened. Coming in as a rookie, one of the guys I competed against on the offensive line, Jim Nicholson (Big Nick) had a completely different attitude. Offensive line mindset is different than that of a defensive line mindset. Offensive line is like a micro team, a team within a team. With Big Nick, during practice we would go head-to-head physically, and then after practice, he would show me different moves and techniques to use on offensive linesmen. Until this day, I know this accelerated my defensive position. All through my high school and college career, I played as an outside linebacker. Now, for the first time ever in my football career, I played in a three-point position directly across from an offensive tackle. Big Nick proved to me the value of team work and respect. He showed how teammates should work together for the benefit of the team. Keep in mind that this is during camp, and no one has a permanent position. He was showing me moves that I could use against him in practice that could possibly jeopardize his position or job.

As you may have noticed, I've been on the receiving end where others, coaches, trainers, parents, teachers, et cetera, have helped me become the person I am today. I have been able to help other teammates during my career as well. Ted McKnight and Tony Reed are a couple of players who have been recipients of not just mine, but Sylvester Hicks' and Don Parrish's assistance. In 1979, Sylvester, Don and I were working undercover for the Jackson County Health Department. Some of the fellas such as Ted and Tony were storing the homemade delicious lunches that were made by their wives in their locker. Being that Don, Sly and I were concerned about their health, we reported it to the Jackson County Health Department. Our assignment? To test each BBQ turkey sandwich or any other item left in their lunch for over an hour. This proved successful, until our cover was blown. How was it blown? Keep in mind, we were sacrificing our stomachs on behalf of our teammates. Toward the end of the season, Ted McKnight had a couple of nice sandwiches and three nice soft chocolate chip cookies. We confiscated the lunch and analyzed its contents. This was on a Wednesday, about two games before the last. We were confronted by Ted in front of all of our teammates and questioned about his missing lunch. As dedicated, undercover officers for the

Health Department, we pleaded the fifth – DENIAL. The victim made the statement, "We will find out if you are telling the truth because those three big, soft chocolate cookies weren't what you thought. The chocolate was replaced with Ex-Lax." Still (no pun intended) we were in DENIAL. After everyone left, Sylvester, Don and myself began to deny who ate them among ourselves. We made it through 2/3 of the practice that day in disbelief, like we were out of the woods. We were standing on the sideline, waiting for our turn, when we heard and felt some rumbles. We looked in the sky, and it was a clear, sunny day. No rain in sight! Then we figured it out – one by one, our denial subsided, as we raced to the one and only Johnny on the Spot! Lesson learned! The entire team, including Coach Levy, turned our way and started laughing. COVER BLOWN! The next three days, all of us were still flowing. Dave Kendall, our trainer, asked Ted how much Ex-Lax his wife put in the cookies. Come to find out, he put one whole block in each cookie. Until this day, Ted has not thanked us for extending his career. The way I look at it is, if we hadn't sacrificed our stomachs and eaten those lunches, he probably would've been moved to offensive lineman. I would like to officially thank Ted for almost a whole season of free lunches and the free colonic that came along with it. Thank you, Ted, and you are welcome.

As a young one in high school, all of the guys I played with had a player they idolized or mimicked. My nickname at Camden High School was the Mad Stork. I mentioned earlier that the Raiders were my favorite team. The Mad Stork, Ted Hendricks, was 6'7" and number 83. My height in high school was 6'7" and my number was 83. We both were outside linebackers. If you look at my varsity letter jacket, it has "Mad Stork, #83" on it. One of the highlights of my entire career in the NFL is playing in the Pro Bowl in my three-point stance, side by side, with Ted Hendricks – Big Mad Stork and Little Mad Stork, me.

I realize that my mother, Coach Andy Hinson, Fran Curci, Marv Levy, John Mackovic and Frank Gansz, along with all the assistant coaches who coached me over the years, had different methodologies of coaching, but had one key ingredient: RESPECT. As my mother always reminded me, "Weed out the negatives and focus on taking the positives."

I truly believe that I was very fortunate to have this solid foundation. Through vision, heart, and soul, I was devoted to creating an environment for members of my team along with myself to thrive outside of our surroundings. The ultimate goal is to be able to catch fish on our own in this world and pass it on. "A good coach can change a game; a great coach can change a life." – John Wooden

As we understand and appreciate how important respect is, it takes us to an additional important ingredient that will assist us in becoming not only a successful student athlete (notice STUDENT), but more importantly, young adults in our communities. Those ingredients are team concept, discipline, structure, perseverance, developing good habits, and setting goals.

As Vince Lombardi said, coaches who win get inside their players and motivate. Athletes need to believe in you, see and feel your passion, know you are there for them, that they are your priority. So, what do my mother and Coach Vince Lombardi have in common? RESPECT for others no matter what age, talent, shade, et cetera. The old saying is "in order to get respect you have to give respect!" That respect comes from your parents or coaches, and it also comes in the means of training, to act in accordance with rules; drills equal Discipline.

Over the years, I have developed a bad case of chronic figurative tinnitus and the root cause, my mother. This ringing sound was and still is a constant all through the day, every day, and what I have found in LIFE is that the key to any of my relationships is this: Be respectful, responsible and accountable for my actions. What was emphasized by my mother was that these are action words, and you don't just say them, you live them!

About Art Still

Art Still is a writer, speaker and CEO of Still 4 Life, an e-commerce business that believes in "paying it forward."

He was born and raised in Camden, New Jersey, where he graduated from Camden High School in 1974.

Art was a four-year starter at the University of Kentucky, where he was named SEC Player of the Year and Consensus All-American as a senior. He was inducted into the College Football Hall of Fame in 2015.

In 1978, Art was the first-round draft pick of the Kansas City Chiefs and played 12 seasons in the NFL with the Chiefs and Buffalo Bills. He was selected to four Pro Bowls, was a two-time MVP, and inducted into the Kansas City Chiefs Hall of Fame in 1997.

In addition to a very active family life, Art has taken on various projects since he left the game, including charity work with several organizations. Still remains connected with football, serving as one of the Kansas City Chiefs' ambassadors. In that role, he is frequently out and about in the community with other former players. "You get an opportunity to work in the community with a variety of charities and groups of people," said Still, who has been married to wife Liz since 1983. "We enjoy doing things that are positive and something that will be lasting in helping others. We do a lot of benefits and working with youths and their families."

Chapter 5

12 Tips for Improved Athletic Performance

By David Justice

Growing up, baseball always came easy to me. I wasn't particularly athletic when it came to the basic tenets of running, jumping, and changing directions, but I could always hit and throw a baseball better than most of my peers. By the time I got to high school, I'd never really faced any adversity within the sport. Little did I know, that was about to change – my sophomore and junior seasons proved to be two of the most difficult years of my life, both on *and* off the field.

Regardless of how talented you are, there will come a day when you're no longer the best one out on the field. Whether that happens in little league or Major League Baseball, it will hurt just the same. And while I learned that lesson the hard way during my first year on varsity, the experience taught me a lot about how to prepare myself physically and mentally in order to put myself in the best possible position to succeed. Below are the lessons I learned during that time.

Physical:

1. **Eat more**

   Isaac Newton's Second Law of Motion states that Force = Mass x Acceleration. Why am I starting off with a Physics lesson when that was literally the only C I got in all of high school? Because it's relevant. The bigger you are (*mass*), the harder you will be able to throw (*force*). While this doesn't mean that all 6'4" 230 lb. pitchers should be throwing 96 miles per hour, chances are it does apply to you. When you gain weight, you're increasing your mass.

   Multiply the added weight to the acceleration you had been producing previously, the force on the other end of the equation goes up. That's not theoretical – that's simply the math of how things work out in this regard.

   Here's a recent tweet from Eric Cressey of Cressey Sports Performance: "22 MLB pitchers w/ 30+ IP this year have average fastball velos of 97+ mph. Only 3/22 are under 200 lbs. If you're sick of throwing 77 mph, EAT."

Rule of Thumb: Most teenagers have metabolism rates that are absolutely through the roof, which means they need to eat more than the average person in order to maintain/gain weight. Try Googling "how many calories do I need to eat per day in order to go from ABC pounds to XYX pounds" and use one of the calculators that comes up from the search results. It will vary from person to person and will also factor in the amount of physical activity you're currently subjected to.

2. Recover better

Sleep More

Getting teenagers (and even many adults) to go to bed at a reasonable hour has always been a tough thing to do. Now throw in smart phones, tablets, and laptops to the mix, and that exacerbates the problem even further. Unfortunately, not getting enough sleep has proven to be detrimental to an individual's ability to function at a high level both physically and mentally.

The research journal *SLEEP* recently conducted a study that revealed that an individual with inadequate levels of sleep "show declines in split-second decision making" while well-rested individuals "showed increased accuracy" under the same testing protocol. Further, their research shows that that a lack of sleep leads to "the possibility of fatigue, low energy, and poor focus at game time."

Rule of Thumb: Depending on who you ask, you'll likely get a wide range of responses as far as recommendations for how many hours you should be sleeping each night. Some believe that teenagers and young adults require nine plus hours per night, but that's difficult to achieve in this day and age. As a general rule of thumb, I'd say shoot for seven-nine hours, and figure out what works best for *you*.

Drink More Water

The human body is composed of roughly 60% water, which means it's pretty darn important. In fact, even under the most dire circumstances, you would need water several days before needing food in a do-or-die situation.

What role does proper hydration play in relation to the body's functions, you ask?

First, it regulates your core body temperature. In instances where you haven't been drinking enough water, your body will start to overheat, which puts hefty amounts of stress on the body's energy systems and vital organs. When your body is working overtime just to regulate its temperature, this will in turn negatively affect both your performance on the field and your recovery off it.

Second, proper hydration helps to regulate your blood pressure. This in turn promotes a steady and consistent heart rate, which keeps the physical stress internally to a minimum. When not kept in check, elevated blood pressure leads to inflammation and additional processes that hurt your performance and recovery.

The third and final component is that proper hydration assists in the movement and transport of essential energy nutrients such as proteins, carbohydrates and fats which the body uses as fuel and sustenance. When you've drank sufficient amounts of water, these processes are far more efficient and less taxing on your body than otherwise, which then elevates your performance on the field and maximizes recovery afterwards.

Rule of Thumb:

- Before Exercise
    - 1-2 hours: 8-16 oz. of cold water
    - 10 15 minutes: 8-12 oz.
- During Exercise
    - 5-10 oz. every 20 minutes
- After Exercise:
    - Within two hours: at least 24 oz.

3. Play multiple sports

In order to be the best you can be at your chosen sport, you need to maximize your potential as an athlete. For a baseball player, that doesn't necessarily mean fielding hundreds of ground balls or spending hours in the batting cage – although your coaches will definitely love that work ethic! What it means is playing other sports during the off-season – like football, basketball, or soccer, to name a few – that challenge your body in different ways than baseball does.

Think about it for a minute. The four sports mentioned above are fundamentally different from one another in a variety of ways. If you only play baseball year round, you aren't really exposed to the starting, stopping, jumping, and changing of direction that you'll see out on the basketball court. If you spend time during the off-season improving on skills that are front and center in your sport of choice, you will notice improvements in aspects of your game such as base running, ability to change directions out in the field, and your overall conditioning and levels of athleticism.

Rule of Thumb: Play another sport during your primary sport's off-season, even if it's just for fun. I was never very good at basketball, but I started playing in the local rec league in middle school, and continued playing through the end of high school. I loved every minute of it. Not only was it great for keeping me in shape for baseball, it's an awesome way to let off some steam if you're a competitive person.

4. **Make the most of your off-season**

Here's that age-old "do as I say, not as I do" segment in today's blog for you.

I remember back when I was 16, 17, 18 years old and trying to get recruited to play baseball at the D1 level. Every year, I would play the spring season for my school, the summer season for a traveling team, and the fall season with another traveling squad. I always felt like if I took one season off, either my abilities as a baseball player or my chances to get recruited would fall off a cliff. Looking back now, neither one would have occurred and my body would've thanked me for the additional time off.

In the 10+ years since I graduated high school, training baseball players has come a long way. Between more concentrated workout routines, stricter pitch count limits, and an increased level of understanding of the role that proper nutrition and recovery plays, it's night and day compared to what things used to be. After an epidemic of Tommy John surgeries and shoulder issues, we as an industry have discovered better ways to prepare baseball players both on the field and behind the scenes in places like the weight room.

We've also learned that less is more when it comes to throwing. If you're a pitcher, don't be afraid to take three to four months off from throwing during the fall and early winter to give your arm time to recover from the beating it took during the spring and summer months. You won't magically forget how to throw hard. If anything, you'll come back throwing harder the next season, if you've done your due diligence and spent the off-season doing productive things like eating right, working out, and getting enough sleep.

Rule of Thumb: Spend the off-season away from your sport. Either play another sport, and/or spend the time in the weight room working on getting bigger/stronger/faster in preparation for next season. Focus on eating right, drinking enough water, and getting enough sleep as well.

5. **Know when to back off**

There's a difference between pain and injury. Figure out what your threshold for pain is and what you're comfortable dealing with. If it's the off-season and you tweak something, it's probably not going to be a big deal.

Shut it down for a few days or weeks if necessary and come back 100% ready to go. If something happens in-season during a practice or game, you may or may not be able to play through it. Talk to your athletic trainer or doctor for their advice, and then give it a go if you're up for it.

Mental:

6. **Set goals**

   Have you ever noticed how you tend to be more successful when you have an idea of what it is you're hoping to accomplish? This is likely because you set a goal, which allowed you to put together a mental roadmap to follow to help reach your goal. With that in mind, the best way to stay on track and not lose focus in your endeavors is to set SMART goals. SMART goals are:

   - Specific – very clearly defined
   - Measurable – you can quantify your progress along the way
   - Attainable – challenging, but not impossible
   - Realistic – it has to be doable one way or another
   - Timely – there is an end date by which you intend to accomplish said goal

Bad example: I want to be a better baseball player.

Good example: Next season, I want to hit .300 or above and lead my team in RBIs. I will accomplish this by continuing to attend my weekly hitting lessons with my instructor, along with performing my off-season workout routine three days a week in order to continue improving my strength and hand-eye coordination.

7. **Trust the process**

Your coaches have their jobs for a reason. This applies to the coach of your school team, whoever you go to for private lessons, and even your strength and conditioning coach. Chances are they played your sport in high school, and maybe even college, so they likely know what they're talking about.

It's easy to get caught up in the mindset that you or your parents know best all the time. However, give your coach the benefit of the doubt. If they suggest slight mechanical adjustments or different ways of doing things, give it a shot. It's in their best interest that you do well, so they won't be doing anything to lead you astray. Or if you don't understand why certain exercises are included in your routine, just ask. Your strength coach will gladly explain the reason behind every single component of your workouts and why they are included in order to help you accomplish your goals on the field.

8. Always be on time

My high school coach operated under the following philosophy: "If you're five minutes early, you're on time. If you're on time, you're late." He preached that message relentlessly during the time I played for him, and it still rings clear after all these years.

It doesn't matter what I'm doing or where I'm going, I'm always early. And I'm proud of that, too. Nothing bothers me more than people who can't figure out how to be on time for anything. It's disrespectful of other people's time, and quite frankly, it's selfish. If you make a commitment to somebody, the least you can do is value their time enough to meet them when you said you would.

9. Practice smarter

Practice isn't always fun. In fact, that's rarely the case. But as you get older and continue progressing to more advanced levels of competition, you begin to see that the best players are oftentimes the ones who make the most of their time during practice. The best part about this one is that you don't have to be supremely talented to get an edge on the competition. All that really matters is that you pay attention to what it is your coaches are teaching on any given day and then go out and execute to perfection.

As Vince Lombardi famously said, "Practice does not make perfect. Only perfect practice makes perfect."

10. Be a team player

If you didn't notice, I talk about baseball a lot because that's what I know best. I'm going to give another example here from a situation in my past that occurred the summer before my senior year of high school on my summer traveling team.

Back in 2006, I was fortunate enough to play on the 18-U KC Sluggers team while I was still 17, because one of the catchers on that team had quit at the last minute. While I was ecstatic about playing with teammates who were a year older than me, I had also just completed my first season on varsity and was in the midst of an abysmal slump at the plate. That slump continued throughout the summer and into that fall, and it wasn't until late in the year that I got things turned around.

But the moral of the story is this – I knew I wasn't hitting well, but I couldn't figure out why. So instead of dwelling on the negative, I made it my mission to help my team compete any way possible.

As a result, two major developments came out of that year. First, I improved my defensive skills as a catcher by a landslide. Second, I learned how to bunt with the best of them. While the former was more of a landmark accomplishment for my baseball career (and was a major reason why I was offered a scholarship to play at Northwest Missouri State), the latter was the one I cared more about at the time. You see, I had hit in the 3-hole my entire life dating back to coach-pitch softball in kindergarten. That was always what I did – I hit the ball really, really hard. But when I came face-to-face with a season-long slump, I acquired a new skill, bunting, and took advantage of it early and often because that was the best way –at least offensively – that I could help my team win.

11. Be resilient

While #10 is an example of being resilient, I'm going to use another story from my life's experiences to help illustrate this one.

As I previously mentioned, baseball came pretty easily to me growing up. Going into tryouts during my sophomore year of high school, I honestly believed that I'd be the backup catcher on varsity.

Unfortunately, my coach had other plans. I spent the entire season on JV and was silently fuming for months about the fact that I had been left off the varsity roster for a team that ended up making a run at the state title. Now, I did end up having a very successful season on the field and was proud of my accomplishments. But I never did forget the perceived slight that I wasn't good enough to at least sit on the bench during varsity games.

What did I do about it? Well, I'll begin by telling you the JV season ended after a Saturday morning doubleheader against Olathe Northwest at CBAC (we lost both games). Monday morning, I told my dad I wanted to get serious about working out. He showed me a well-rounded routine that would help me get bigger and stronger, and the rest is history.

Over the course of the next nine months, I gained nearly 30 lbs. of muscle and completely revamped my body composition. While I knew that I would've been on varsity my junior season regardless of the circumstances, I wanted to put no doubt in my coach's mind that I was physically ready to play at that level. After beginning the following season as the starting first baseman and backup catcher, I worked my way into the starting catcher role four-five games into the season, and we ended up making a return trip to the state tournament.

Quite simply, if you want something bad enough, you have to go and get it. Bad things will happen. How you respond makes all the difference.

12. Think less

I won't spend a ton of time on this one, because it doesn't take much to get my point across. You've spent countless hours practicing and preparing for game time – trust your instincts. Trust your muscle memory. Trust what you've learned.

One of my biggest issues with the season-long slump in 2006 was the fact that it wasn't the ability of the pitchers on varsity that caused my problems. I was merely overthinking **everything**. I had started going to a new hitting instructor the winter before and he had made *just* enough adjustments that I was thinking instead of doing every single time I swung the bat. The resulting scenario was an embarrassing mess. It took me far too long to get back to the basics, and remember that what I had been doing the previous 10-12 years had been working just fine and that there was no reason to change.

I finally snapped out of it, but I count that as the lost year of my baseball career. Try to learn from my mistakes so it doesn't happen to you.

About David Justice

David Justice has been involved in the fitness industry since he started at AYC Health & Fitness as a personal trainer in August of 2014. Since then, he has trained hundreds of individuals of all ages and ability levels and has spent a great deal of time specializing in working with youth athletes, particularly baseball players. He credits the experience of gaining 25 pounds of muscle between his sophomore and junior year in high school as the inspiration behind going into this career path. The numerous benefits, both physical and mental, of that experience turned into a passion for exercise that he would like to pass on to as many people as possible.

Chapter 6

The Power of Performance

By Joe Drake

I can remember sitting there crying and thinking, "What do I do now?"

In the grand scheme of life, it wasn't that bad, and I knew it was coming, but it still felt like part of me was getting thrown away.

It was my last game of high school football, and for as long as I could remember, I was an athlete. I played three to four sports almost my entire life, and I couldn't really fathom what life was going to be like without it.

It's where I tested myself and learned about resolve and commitment. It's where I built an understanding of self-awareness and confidence. It's how I learned to compete and challenge the people around me. It's where I felt like I was truly myself, and now it was coming to an end.

I was never an outwardly emotional guy, but as Coach Valadez came up to me after the game, tears streaming down his face and telling me that he was proud of me, I couldn't hold it in. I just lost it.

It had become so intertwined with how I saw myself and my identity that I wasn't sure who I was without sports. When I wasn't training, I didn't feel like the same person, and I wasn't nearly as happy. I was excited about college and what lay ahead, but that scared the hell out of me. Call it a blessing or a curse, but I had been brought up in an environment where working hard to get better was mandatory, and I had grown to like it that way.

From doing pushups and sit-ups in between commercials to spending hours hitting lima beans with my dad in the basement for batting practice, it was about taking advantage of every opportunity to get better and holding myself to a higher standard than those around me.

Outwork everyone. Maximize your potential.
Don't accept mediocrity. Play to win.

My entire life revolved around preparing for the next sport, and then playing it. I truly loved not only competing, but training. I noticed early on that when I was physically dialed in, it was easier to get the rest of my life in sync.

Too many people walk around like victims wondering why they aren't achieving their dreams, yet they have no physical or mental routine to keep them focused and on path. Then there are some who may actually achieve great success in their career, yet do so to the detriment of their body, and vice versa. Little do most know that growth, in any aspect of life, requires the exact same set of skills, focus, and mindset.

There's something innately human about performance and achievement. It goes beyond just physical performance and sports into a place of fulfilling a deeper calling and purpose. It is a deep-seated, even if unspoken, desire to become something more than what we currently are. Call it legacy or curiosity, but regardless, that little voice lives inside of all of us asking, *"If I were to really stretch myself, what am I actually capable of?"*

"Am I actually stretching myself?"

"Where does that line of impossibility and unrealistic exist for me, and am I willing to push it?"

"What will be my legacy for the world?"

What determines how far we take things is our desire to explore the answer. Far too many people silence that voice in their lives and stop asking themselves those questions.

It might start with no longer competing in athletics or not striving to crush an exam, but then before you know it, that voice that used to make you question your limits falls silent in other areas of life. We get used to being comfortable, and we lose our edge.

But that's not where personal progress lies, and I kind of like having that little voice around.

Like many former athletes out of high school and college with an abundance of unstructured time, I poured myself into the gym. I was no longer competing on the field, but I enjoyed training like I was. I was on a mission and focused. In the chaos of daily life and dealing with my transition into adulthood, it seemed like the one thing I could truly control. You put in the work day after day, and you can physically see and feel the results.

This positive feedback loop elevated my confidence in a way I hadn't expected. It mentally opened up more possibility to me across the board. It encouraged me to see myself not as I was, but what I could become. The more I embraced physical challenge, the more comfortable I was with stretching myself mentally and spiritually.

At the time, I had no idea where it would lead me, but when I became conscious of the impact that my performance training lifestyle and approach was having on my growth, I knew my life had to be dedicated to sharing it with others.

This is what led me to my first job in fitness, working the front desk at a 24 Hour Fitness. I can still remember what went through my mind the first time James came up to the desk. I thought to myself, "How is this guy going to get around the gym safely with nobody on him the entire time?"

James was blind, and he had joined a gym for the first time in his life. He was in his late twenties and a little bit shy as he made his way into the gym, but he just wanted to be shown how to work the treadmill and maybe a couple of machines. I spent time making sure he knew exactly where everything was and how to use it. Then I got out of his way and let him get after it.

James came in like clockwork three times a week and hopped onto the treadmill to start his workout. In the first few weeks it was a fast walk, but before I knew it, I looked over and James was running full tilt on the treadmill. I ran over to him to check on him and he slowed the machine down, full smile on his face and said, "I didn't think I'd be able to do that, but what do you know?"

From then on, it was a run and not a walk.

The next time he came in, James asked me to show him some more machines. I noticed James came in with a different walk and confident posture than when I first met him. He was chatting up people when he was out on the floor, making friends, and we kept adding weight to the exercises he was doing. His body was changing right in front of me and along with it, his confidence. This went on for about six months and then one day as he was getting off of the treadmill he said, "Joe, I think I'm going to try and learn to play baseball."

I chuckled a little bit and shook my head while I told him to stop messing with me. He didn't even crack a smile.

This guy was serious!

I was blown away. Here was a guy who walked in never having worked out before, not to mention had absolutely no sight, and months later had proved to himself what he was capable of, and wanted to take on more. I hadn't even worked with James as a trainer or coach, but observing what happened to him in a matter of months was enough for me to know there was something about physical achievement that could unlock other areas of our life.

Fast forward ten years, and I have had the chance to work with hundreds of people on their health, fitness, and training goals. I have seen people along the way make life-changing shifts, but have seen even more fall short.

So what's the magic equation? What is it that seems to separate those who are able to achieve such great things and make massive progress from those who aren't able to make it click?

The last decade has led me to believe that the common thread connecting the perpetually successful can be found inside of their approach towards life. There are no special strategies or tricks to get there quickly. All of it is tied to a mindset of performance that's both physical and mental. This way of life may come easier to some, but it is absolutely reproducible.

It's what drives someone to wake up and swim thousands of meters a day at Masters Swim, just to prove to themselves that they can. It's also what pushes someone to sacrifice years of their life to developing a new company or product. Some people just seemed to be wired for it, but it all comes down to behaviors and focus. Thankfully, for all of us, it can (and must) be learned and developed if we are looking for greater than average results in our life.

What follows are four key factors to focus on when developing an unstoppable Performance Mindset. They will take time and are often uncomfortable, but within each of them lies the key to conquering whatever goals or challenges lie ahead.

Top Four tips for Engaging in the Performance Mindset

[1] Embrace the Suck

I prefer to take a hopeful approach towards humanity and believe in the power of people, but I have also come to realize that often, we are walking contradictions. Think about it for a second. What area of your life do you know that you need to work on or take action in, but you continue to put it on the back burner?

I have no problem using myself as an example. I decided to pursue my life's purpose as a Fitness Professional and Health Coach. This means I made the conscious decision to be an icon of health and fitness for others.

I love it, and I couldn't imagine doing anything else with my life. *However, I went four years without health care insurance.* Thankfully, it was a healthy time of my life, and I had no emergencies or need to see a doctor, but here I was telling people to get regular check-ups and take care of their bodies, yet I was not walking the walk. I wanted the title without the sacrifice.

Now, I believe all of us have little areas of our lives where our words don't always match our actions. I don't think it makes anyone dishonest, but those who perform at a high level and continue to succeed match their words with their actions to a greater degree than the rest.

106

One of my favorite football players growing up was Jerry Rice. I remember hearing at a young age about his brutal work ethic and off-season workouts that other players in the league couldn't even complete. He was running sprints after practice and training six days a week once the season ended. Nobody else was doing that.

Jerry did, and it's why he was the best. This wasn't a one-time thing, but the type of training routine that he maintained throughout his twenty-year career in the league.

Rice was undoubtedly talented, but was he an athletic anomaly? No. What set him apart was his ability to embrace the unbearably hard work needed to get better when his teammates and competitors were taking time off. He knew it wasn't the fun stuff that would make him a legend, and he took it head on.

It's kind of like losing weight…

What does it really take to change your body and lose weight? Is it really that complicated? Not at all. Actually, for most people the path is easily defined.

I won't downplay the psychological challenges that many people face in the process, but in all reality, it's not an unknown route. The challenges are inside of us, not out in the real world. It's just REALLY tough to stay patient, consistent, and motivated long enough to see it through.

Playing the long game isn't sexy, and we want results yesterday. This creates unhappiness with the process, and I believe is one of the main reasons people struggle to stay the course.

Whether you are struggling to make progress in your body, professional life, or relationships, the skills and steps are generally the same. It comes down to the ability to delay gratification and embrace discomfort as an essential part of achievement. If you're looking to take on something new, try leaning into the struggle instead of avoiding it and it could just become your secret weapon.

#embracethesuck

[2] Run with the wolves

"I want you to go find the best guy on the court and guard him."

I'll never forget my father telling me this when we went to go play pick-up basketball at the YMCA when I was in middle school. Here I am, sneaking into open gym at an age when I'm not even supposed to be on the court, and he's telling me to try and guard guys who played at a college level.

I thought he was crazy at the time, but I can never thank my father enough for making me compete on a level beyond my comfort zone. Whether it meant lying about my age to get me onto an older team or encouraging me to apply for

Harvard, he pushed me to put myself around those who were leaps and bounds ahead of me.

Going this route doesn't always feel good, but is a sure-fire way to get better fast. I remember the first time I came back from a high-level fitness mastermind group. My partner and I had opened up our facility, Gravity + Oxygen Fitness, and were making progress. I decided to invest in becoming part of a group of other gym owners and entrepreneurs from around the country. I gained a lot of insight while I was there and although the event was inspiring, I came back mad. Not because of things we were doing wrong, but because I wasn't thinking big enough. The group opened my eyes to what was truly possible and made me be honest about how much I was truly stretching myself.

I didn't enjoy feeling inadequate, but you can bet it forced me to make massive progress in the coming year. Maybe it was a little bit of friendly competition, but it was also being around those who are further down the path. It motivated me to get to thc next level, and many of us are like this.

If you're the best player on the court, then people will continue to play to your level; but if you're not the best, then you're likely to find a way to play beyond your current abilities. I saw it work against some of my most athletically-gifted friends growing up. They developed quickly, but continued to play sports with kids their own age and weren't challenged enough. Over time, the rest of us caught up, and they struggled mentally with not being the best anymore. What if they had started playing with others on their level and been challenged more early on?

Most people are familiar with the idea that you'll become most like the people you surround yourself with, but it happens on more levels than you'd think. Not only will you walk and talk like the people around you, but you'll start to think like them. Physical development is one thing, but the magic is in what's also going on upstairs. Developing the mental fortitude and toughness it takes to handle failure and drive long-term progress means surrounding yourself with those who will force you to grow.

Want to be one of the best in your sport? Then you had better find a way to train with the best. Want to be more positive and successful in other areas of life? Make sure to put yourself around the right kind of hungry people who are closer to where you want to be.

Take a look around you and be honest with yourself, if you're putting yourself in the right rooms. Seek out the presence of those who will keep you honest and afraid to get too comfortable. If you're doing it right, it may be with people who occasionally frustrate you and push your buttons. They might even call you out now and again. Being around them may make you feel like you need to step things up and start thinking on their level. Good.

Their role isn't to be your best friend, but to hold your feet to the fire when you need it. Get around these kinds of people and make sure to return the favor. In the end you'll both be better for it.

[3] Find a Coach

Michael Jordan without Dean Smith. Serena and Venus Williams without their father. Who would they be if it weren't for the mentors and coaches in their lives?

It's easy to think about athletes and the impact coaching had on them throughout their careers, but the impact of coaching extends to all areas of life. This is why a guy like Tony Robbins, who coaches and develops people all over the world, is worth over $480 million. People need coaching.

It's the key to accessing things in life we have never experienced, and getting to places in our minds we have never gone. Coaching and mentorship is a part of human nature. From the moment we are born until adulthood, we are taking direction and input from our families, teachers, coaches, and loved ones. All of it shapes who we are to become and how we interact with the world.

Some coaching can be self-taught through books, meditation, and more, but at some level, there is a governor on the speed of success and progress from those who go it alone. You tend to be your own greatest limitation, and finding the right coaches can be the key to the next level.

Sometimes it's also not enough to only be accountable to ourselves. This is probably one of the main reasons Personal Trainers and Fitness Coaches even exist. It's not because people need the most technical and perfectly designed workout program, but because they need someone to help keep them accountable and continue to pave the way. We can only be great at so many things in life, and there is value in knowing when you need direction. Great coaches will help you build skills over time and are a requirement for accelerated progress.

When we have our head down in the jungle hacking away at the weeds, we can use an eagle in the sky with a different perspective on the path ahead. They can help us see things that we wouldn't have otherwise and find shortcuts when necessary. Often times they have traveled the road we are on, and you couldn't put a price on the value of their support and guidance.

Most importantly, don't wait until you're struggling to make the move and find a coach. It takes commitment to seek out help when you aren't struggling. It's what the best of the best do in all areas. Think about an area of your life (or body) that you want to improve and grow in over the next

12 months, and start to seek out someone who can help you gain momentum. Motivation to improve tends to be high when we are down, but what if you could apply the same commitment when you're already doing well?

The performance mindset isn't driven by an attitude of being reactive, but in seeking out challenges and creating growth, not waiting for it to happen to you.

[4] Compete Regularly

That feeling. You know the one.

It builds up in the pit of your stomach to a point where you aren't sure if you're nervous or scared. Your heart is about to beat out of your chest, and you just went to the bathroom for the third time in ten minutes. Your palms are a little sweaty and for a second, you question if you're ready for this.

Yes – *that* feeling. The one you get before a big competition or speech. This is what it feels like to try and find your threshold, the feeling of putting yourself out there on the chopping block for all to see.

The fear of failure and ridicule is what prevents so many from reaching their potential. If there's no potential for stumbling, struggling, or falling off the cliff, then there can be no growth. The spirit of the Performance Mindset means getting comfortable with putting yourself in these situations.

Often.

This doesn't mean you need to feel like you are going to hurl and join a race every weekend, but growth requires challenge. Just like the human body, we have to push and challenge ourselves mentally and emotionally if we want to adapt and grow. Like lifting weights, it's going to get uncomfortable and maybe even hurt sometimes, but it's part of the sacrifice required.

When it comes to areas of our life we don't have a lot of confidence or experience in, it's tough not to start thinking, "Well, what if I don't have what it takes?" Learning to battle that inner voice and find comfort in the struggle are keys to becoming more comfortable with testing your performance for all to see.

It's amazing what happens when we go all-in on something and don't give ourselves a way out.

I met and started training Julia when I first moved to Florida in 2010. I had just finished up college and accepted a graduate assistantship at Florida Atlantic University. Julia was the first client I had once I moved down, and one I will never forget.

Julia was focused mostly on weight loss and leading a healthier lifestyle, something she had struggled with her entire life. Julia was consistent and doing great in starting to see progress, but then one day, she came in and told me that she just decided to book a trip. I knew she liked to travel, so I was curious as to where she was off to, and then she told me that she booked a week-long hiking and rafting trip in the Grand Canyon.

I was stoked, but then hit with a wave of fear and concern as she was describing the trip. It was day after day of dangerous and challenging hiking that would have been a struggle for most fit people of any age.

I was not only a little bit scared for her safety, but I found myself thinking, "What if she can't do it?"

Talk about burning the boat in order to take the island! Julia was smarter than me at the time, and she knew herself. She didn't want to fail, but she knew she needed the challenge in her life. She knew that if she spent the money and put it out there that she was going on a trip like this, then it would force her to get her body to the next level.

Julia's focus and drive in our workouts over the next couple of months went through the roof. It was like we kicked into an entirely different gear. Julia lost a significant amount of weight over the next six months as we prepared for the trip of a lifetime, and she proceeded to complete the entire hike with little to no assistance.

There's something special about completing and achieving something when deep down you doubt yourself. She truly wasn't sure if she would be able to finish it, but was willing to take the chance. Next thing I knew after her trip, Julia was even more motivated to see progress and find the next hill to climb.

Julia needed to prove to herself that she was capable of greatness in order to believe it. An easy trip or hike would have never cut it. She put herself in a place where she was forced to either succeed or fail, nothing in between. This trip was her own way of competing, and it gave her the confidence to start approaching life differently. I saw the shift in her and continue to see it in those brave enough to place these kinds of challenges in front of themselves.

Crafting Your Approach

I imagine you probably have a successful friend in your life. Maybe they are a CEO or small business owner, and they train like an animal. Maybe they compete in Ironman Triathlons throughout the year or adventure races. Regardless, they seem to bring this Performance Mindset to all aspects of their lives. They train, love, and work with the same intensity and focus. Not everyone approaches life this way, but what if creating a consistent mindset approach across the board is the key to accessing more of ourselves?

In 10 years of working one-on-one with clients of all types, the people who continually succeed in reaching their goals create synergy in their lives, rather than separation. They bring the same person to the plate every time they go to bat, and they do so with the same mindset. For me, personally, this has been everything, and I felt lost until figuring it out. How could I still live my life with this driven Performance Mindset without practices and games?

I knew what it was like to compete and succeed in my life when I was an athlete, but it wasn't until I was forced to figure it out on my own that I really made use of the Four Keys, above, to drive growth. Having to learn how it all fit into my life, without athletics there as my base, was the best thing that ever happened to me. Sometimes you have to feel a little bit lost in order to be found.

It's not about learning just a few tips to lose fat, become a better parent, or be more efficient at work. It's about aligning everything in your life to all be moving in the same direction. It's about finding that flow, where taking care of your body pushes you to excel in other areas of your life and build momentum in a never-ending cycle of improvement and fulfillment that can take you anywhere.

It might not be easy, but thankfully, it's also not that complicated. It all starts with an understanding of what it takes and commitment to the process. Focus regularly on the Four Keys described here, and continue to revisit your progress on each of them throughout the next six to twelve months. Start to put pen to paper on where you'd like to see yourself grow and stretch yourself, and you will undoubtedly be on the path to an unstoppable Performance Mindset.

.....Now go get to work!

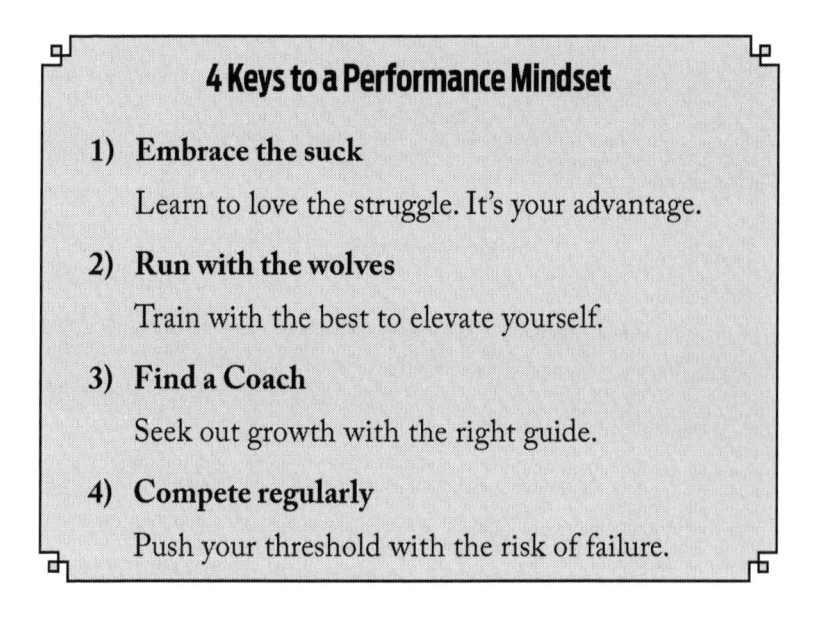

4 Keys to a Performance Mindset

1) **Embrace the suck**

   Learn to love the struggle. It's your advantage.

2) **Run with the wolves**

   Train with the best to elevate yourself.

3) **Find a Coach**

   Seek out growth with the right guide.

4) **Compete regularly**

   Push your threshold with the risk of failure.

About Joe Drake

Joe Drake is co-owner of Gravity + Oxygen Fitness, a successful training studio in Boca Raton, FL. Joe is also co-owner of the Axiom Fitness Academy, where he works closely with new fitness professionals to go from getting certified to finding success in a competitive fitness market. He has worked with a variety of clientele, from professional athletes to special populations and uses his experience with people as he works as a Technogym Senior Master Trainer in the fitness education space.

At his core, Joe is a motivator and educator who is passionate about empowering others to make an impact. When Joe isn't working with his team or other fitness pros from around the country, you can probably find him on a paddleboard with his wife Megan enjoying the South Florida sun. You can connect with him more at www.JoeDrake.com

Chapter 7

Life Lessons

By Jenn Waller

In the process of compiling this book, Joe Drake said, "When you stop competing in sport, you stop competing in life." Nothing could be truer for me.

I grew up playing softball and soccer. I was fortunate to have wonderful, supportive coaches, who found positive ways to help me push myself to be the best I could be. I played through college and university managing both seasons, as well as working and putting myself through school. I think it was the schedule, the predictability and my competitive nature that kept me strong in sports and strong in life.

However, life changed quickly. I was just finishing my last year of junior ball and found out I was pregnant. I was in the best shape of my life, had a great job and everything was exactly as I thought life would be. Although it wasn't my original plan, I was excited, nervous and everything else a soon-to-be mom would be.

My son was born, and although my life changed in an unexpected way, being a mom made it even better. I was able to play my next soccer season after he was born. After I had my second son two years later, however, I became a full-time mom. That was when all those little things that I didn't think were a big deal started falling away; soccer, softball, going to the gym, taking care of myself, coffee with friends.

Having two kids by the age of 28 was both pure love and incredible isolation. My friends were all starting their careers, and although I loved every single part of being a mom, I found myself incredibly lonely.

During that time, my husband and I began our journey through hell. He was diagnosed with mental illness, and we struggled to work through that with two young kids. We found ourselves even more isolated and in an extreme amount of debt. He wasn't working, and I had completely withdrawn from everything. Looking back, I am sure I must have been depressed.

Unfortunately, part of what my husband went through involved self-harm, and I did everything I could to protect the kids and myself from the impact. Despite my best efforts, it slowly etched away at me, and I completely lost myself. I put on weight. My self-confidence disappeared. I resented life and found myself working three jobs to support our family.

One of my side jobs was as a personal trainer. It was something that I had loved to do, but felt with my weight and lack of my own activity in sports and fitness, I had no right to be doing it. Fortunately, I had a few clients who refused to let me stop training them, so I kept going.

One spring, I had a client who really wanted to try a sprint triathlon. As I felt any good trainer would, I committed to training with her. About a month into training, she broke her foot at work and was unable to complete that goal. Although she couldn't compete in the race like we planned, I committed to completing the goal.

The honest truth was that I kept training my clients, but didn't really follow through on my own training. I judged myself and kept asking myself why everyone else could go to the gym, work out and work towards their goals, but I was so empty. I wanted to do the race, but had no motivation to actually train. At the same time, I so desperately wanted to in my own head. I just didn't know why I was stuck. Have you ever experienced something that like? You want it so bad in your head, but you just can't get going? If you have, then you can relate to how frustrated and lost I felt.

Race Day came, and the good news is, I did it. The bad news is, I did it by the seat of my pants. My time was terrible. I struggled through the whole thing. My attitude was that I was punishing myself for not training properly, and that I deserved to be in the pain I was in. The only positive in the race was when my son, who was 10 at the time, ran the last 400 m or so to the finish line with me.

I learned many lessons from that race.

Lesson #1: Your kids look up to you

He didn't see the time. He saw a mom who finished and did something big.

Lesson #2: Great things are possible with effort

You may be able to do things and fly by the seat of your pants, but great things are possible. I didn't quite believe this right away, but I kept thinking, "If I can do that without training properly, what is possible if I put energy and effort into it?"

Lesson #3: I don't need to punish my body

My body is capable of many amazing things, and treating it like garbage and approaching any race or training session as a punishment is not a way to care for myself.

Reflecting on that experience, I realized how much I had given up. I realized that I was slowly withdrawing from anything that meant anything. I no longer had purpose for me, and could only define myself as a wife and mother. I was going through the motions of life and had stopped fighting for anything of value.

Despite these realizations, life didn't fully change for me in that moment. It continued to spiral and things got worse. I was working 80+ hours a week, my husband was struggling with his mental health, and debts were piling up beyond anything we could control. The only exercise I was getting was driving my kids to the rink and helping my youngest get dressed for his hockey games. Life lacked meaning. I lacked meaning and purpose. I doubted I could accomplish anything. I got complacent and stopped trying again. I was going through the motions of life, struggling with depression and not fully aware of what was happening.

The lowest moment came when my husband decided he no longer wanted to be married. He wasn't doing well, and he changed the locks on my home. In an instant, I was homeless. Worse yet, he was trying to keep me from my children. I crumbled. I felt I had no resources and nowhere to go. My life had no meaning, and it would have been easy to disappear.

I had to decide, what do I want for me? What do I want for my kids? What can I show my kids?

Perhaps it was the competitor in me, or maybe it was just my stubbornness and pride; all I know is that I had the support from an incredible friend - a friend who saved my life by encouraging me to dig deep within myself and make a choice. I chose to build a new life.

Back to lesson #1...

My kids look up to me. Who do I want to be for them? What do I want to demonstrate to them? What do I want to teach them about how to handle the ups and downs of life?

I had to dig deep, and what I realized was that I was at my best in life when I was participating in sports. In those moments, my life always made sense, too. So, I decided that my goal would be to complete an Olympic distance Triathlon. Why? Because for the first time in my life I needed to compete for me. I needed to show up for me, to train for me, to find that internal motivation. I always showed up for soccer and softball because I would never let my team down, this time I had to do it to not let *me* down.

I also knew the goal had to be bigger than a sprint triathlon. I had already proven that I could do that, by the seat of my pants. I needed to pick something bigger, something scarier, and something that would require work.

Lesson #2: What happens if I put energy into something and don't fly by the seat of my pants?

I started slowly. I hired a coach

Next lesson – going at something really big should never be done alone. In order to stop punishing myself for where I was, I had to learn to exercise and train as a way of respecting my body.

I completed one workout after another. As the workouts slowly started falling into place, so did the pieces of my life. Just like I did with my training, I started over in my life. I identified a starting point, and started going upwards from there.

Of course, I had to become vulnerable in a way I had never opened up before. I had to tell people what was happening – that my marriage fell apart, that I had nowhere to go. I had to tell coaches and friends that I had a big goal, but was out of shape and starting at the beginning. You have no idea what an incredibly difficult step this was for me. I had always been in isolation and silence with the scary, unpredictable life I was living. Speaking up and saying anything that was happening was never safe, it carried a huge risk, so being silent just became easy.

It was a year of building, a year of hard work, a year of putting my life together, and a year of putting a goal together. Finally, the big day came – an Olympic distance race in Calgary.

The morning in Calgary was chilly, and I couldn't help but feel nervous, as Keri was bringing her dad, Mike, to the race. Keri is the amazing, supportive friend who I mentioned earlier, someone who has stood by my side since the day I was locked out, and been the most important person in my life, supporting and encouraging me. She is someone I am honored to now call my partner in life. Mike was happily coming out to support me. It made me feel good, and at the same time, my nervousness made my stomach turn.

I went ahead of them to clear my head and get myself set up. I grabbed my Tim's (Tim Horton's is a coffee staple in Canada) in the drive-through, and set off down the highway with the tunes playing. This time allowed me to settle into my pre-race routine.

When I arrived, the course looked good. I kept telling myself that it was fairly flat and the course would be fast. I set myself up like I had done so many times before – talking to people, getting my body marking and setting my fuel on my bike. But this race was different; I was hollow.

For once the lake didn't look intimidating – rather, the opposite. I felt a very unusual calm. This water had nothing on the two previous weeks of rough water I faced with my son. My 14-year-old, my not-so-mini-me, had taken the world on his shoulders, and two years of internal emotional turmoil from the shock of his dad and my separation, and the anger that he was finally starting to voice about how his father treated me. We had been through hell together. It was two painful weeks of slowly unraveling the hurt that he had been feeling, of my being patient and letting him tell his story in his way and his time. We spent a lot of time in silence, which often killed me, but I had to let him be him, and just be present with him and show him that no matter what, he didn't have to "Do" anything to earn my love, that I was there, no matter what, no questions, just because. How do I do that?

Once again, I was snapped out of my thoughts with a gentle touch on the shoulder from Keri, who was wishing me luck, telling me to go after it, telling me that for sure I could hit a personal best.

The call came for all athletes to get in the water. I felt good. I was ready. I was with some really happy and encouraging male competitors; yes, this was a mass start race where all the women and men would start together.

Before I knew it, the gun went off. I stood my ground for a few seconds as the chaos started. Arms and legs were flying everywhere. The guy beside me turned, and we shared a laugh, because neither of us wanted to get swallowed whole by the mass of people leaving the beach. Another deep breath, and I pushed myself into the water. I was three strokes in when there was a sudden jolt to the side of my head and shoulder.

What the heck? I quickly realized that someone had come right in front of me, and I got the full force of their kick to my shoulder - my bad shoulder (the one that had been dislocated just the previous year). Before I could even think, excruciating pain ran through my shoulder, arm, neck and back. Oh, crud, it couldn't have just dislocated again, could it? I kept my legs kicking and found there was no rotation in my shoulder, just a piercing pain. I HAD to keep going! How the hell could I stop? Keri's dad was there, my son was counting on me, how on earth could I complain about my situation?

I did the best I could. I can only imagine how ridiculous I looked out in the water. In fact, I was asked on more than one occasion by the life guard if I needed to be pulled. HELL, NO. I wasn't giving up! After completing one lap, 750 m of the 1500 m course, I was barely below the cut off time, but I still wasn't last. I came around the corner of the second lap, hearing those leading the pack just meters behind me. They were about to get out of the water and start on their bikes, and I was just finishing my first lap! Oh my God, could I do it? I had every reason under the sun to pull myself, and no one would question me. No one. In fact, many would probably say I did more than most by doing as much as I did, but I couldn't. I just couldn't bring myself to give up. It was too much work! It had been months and months of training!

The money spent, the sacrifices by everyone in the family, and the whole trip to Calgary. I knew if I could dig deep, just like I had done when life had fallen apart just a year earlier, I could push through and finish the swim, and once I was out of the water, I knew I could get through the bike and run.

I dug deep, really deep, and completely zoned out to be able to complete that swim. When I reached the end, I had to be helped out of the water. When I got out, I could now feel the pressure of gravity on my shoulder. Without the buoyancy of the water, it was going to hurt.

I don't remember getting my shoes on. I don't remember leaving the transition area. I just remember telling Keri my shoulder was out, that I was going to keep going, and that look on her dad's face, excited, worried and supportive.

I got on my bike, and the pain raged through my body as I leaned my arm forward to take the handle bars. I knew if I could just get that left hand on the bar, I would be okay. I did, I pushed and felt (and heard) a horrible pop in the shoulder. Did it just pop back in? I didn't know. I just knew I had to keep those legs pedaling.

Calgary was a strange course - five laps of the bike, five! Enough to make anyone go insane. Yes, the course was flat, but there was one NASTY hill. As you went downhill, you had to hit the brakes and do a 180° turn. Then you climbed right back up. There was absolutely no way to have any sort of momentum from the downhill portion. My legs were on fire. It hurt, plain and simple. I remembered my game plan from my last talk with Brad, my tri coach. We were keeping it simple, hard on the flat, but taking it back to 75-80% effort on the uphill, so it didn't drain my energy tank, then pour it back on when I got back to the flat. It worked. For the first time, I was passing people and not getting passed. I was passing on the flats as others had to rest from pushing it on the hill. It motivated me. As Brad had told me so many times, "Embrace the suck!" And that's what I did....until I hit my 4th lap. My legs were burning. My shoulder really started getting to me. And I really started to wonder.

For anyone who hasn't raced or hasn't put themselves in a physical challenge for a long period of time, 3.5 hours is a LONG freaking time to be lost in your own head. I questioned everything. My body was starting to give out. I was nailing my bike times; in fact, I was en route to a personal best by about 10 minutes. But I could feel myself slipping away.

Maybe the pain was too great?

Maybe I was being stupid by pushing myself too hard?

Maybe my shoulder was really serious, and I was doing more damage by trying to push through?

So many questions went through my mind.

But then it became so clear. I had my son. I had to show my son that life is going to throw you hard stuff at the worst times, but if you just keep putting one foot in front of the other you can get there. I owed that to him for the week of pain he had endured.

How could I give up?

I had a choice.

I had my body.

I had everything.

How could I give up because it had become a little hard?

I came off that bike to find that, in fact, I had set a personal best on the bike by 12 minutes. HOLY CRAP! 12 minutes!

Now my brain was swimming. I was in the transition, fighting to get my bike shoes off, as my arms had basically become useless. Trying to get my running shoes on, knowing that although my swim had been awful, I had almost completely made up for it on my bike. It wasn't a hilly run course at all! I just had to finish. I just had to finish! Heck, I can do that!

I started out of the transition. My head was ready, but my body had other plans. My legs were cramping. My arm was killing me. Everything hurt, badly. I took a deep breath and walked.

Okay, Jenn, get it together. You know this happens. You know you cramped last time after the bike, and you know you got through it. Slow it down. Walk. Keep walking. Keep the legs moving, and slowly let them ease in to moving. They will loosen. They always do. Count on it!

After a kilometer or two, I started to find my rhythm. It was slow, but hey, I was moving. I ran past a house with a sprinkler turned on so high it came over the sidewalk. The friendly homeowner was cheering us on, obviously setting his hose like that on purpose to bring some relief from the heat. What a great community! This became the norm, house after house. There were words of encouragement, sprinklers spraying, and a city embracing the race. How could you not keep going?

I came through the back half of the first lap, and things were really starting to hurt. This is where your body basically starts saying no, and your brain needs to know who's boss. It starts telling the body, "I've got you. It's going to hurt, but I promise you've got this."

My thoughts were flashing back between my son and me….who am I? Who Am I, now?

My son – oh, my son. How could I not push through? If I failed me, then I would, in turn, fail him.

I headed for that final lap, all odds against me, slower then I wanted to be, but still at a pace to finish before the cut off. How could I not give my all for him? What lessons will he get from me when he sees me finish?

I came around the corner for the second lap desperate to see Keri. I needed that affirmation, that even though I am slow and hurting, she is still there and still behind me. There she was, with her dad cheering me on. She didn't have the time on her mind. She didn't know that I wasn't going to hit my personal best. But she was filled with pride. Pride! Pride that I was doing it in the first place. Pride that I had done the work to get there, even when it wasn't easy. Pride that I wasn't giving up. Pride in who I am. I could see it! No words had to be exchanged.

I made a deal with myself. I would listen to my body and allow it a little rest, as long as I could keep moving. I had 45 minutes to finish, and I knew as long as I could run a part of it, I could do it. So, the discipline of walk 1, run 2 started, and for a while it worked. I hit the 6 km mark, the 7 km, and my legs were really pushing me. I was on track and had to keep moving.

Silly games kept playing in my mind, "You can rest if you can just keep running to that pole. Okay, now you need to just keeping running to that car."

Slowly but surely, the mind games, the memories, the promises and all the work came together. The reality is, I had been through so much in life, so many things I had to battle. This was the metaphor. This was it; just one foot in front of the other. I wasn't about anything other than one foot in front of the other. One step at a time. The finish line may have been out of sight at that moment, but I knew I could get there. It wasn't about finding the pain in the moment. It was about opening my eyes and seeing the beauty of the journey. The journey isn't easy. The journey comes with hills, with setbacks, with pain, but it's better to have the journey than to never try, to never know, to never see the beauty along the road.

I finished that race with a sense of accomplishment that I have never felt before. In the middle of everything, anything is possible, and while I had every reason to stop, I also had every reason to keep going.

Life has a way of showing you what you need when you least expect it.

Sport has a way of showing you who you are and what you need in ways you can never imagine until you are in it.

Life and sports together have shown me that I am capable of so much more than I ever thought possible.

Next step…Ironman!

About Jenn Waller

Jennifer Waller has been a certified personal trainer for the past 18 years and owns Prime Fitness, Inc. in Richmond, BC. She has worked hard to create a unique combination of skills that she utilizes to individualize her training programs. Her creative approach to personal training makes it a fun and energetic experience for her clients. She has clients in all age brackets with all skill levels and she is able to adapt to each client on a personal level.

Jenn's areas of specialty include weight loss and transformation, youth, sports performance, and the psychological aspect of physical activity. She holds certificates in Fundamental Movement Patterns, Emotion Focused Therapy, and Powell Transformation. Jenn has specific certification for TWF Level

2, Youth Fit, TRX, Twist Conditioning, and Keiser Cycling. She is working towards her certification in Pound. She has diplomas in Recreation Leadership, Coaching and Instruction, and Exercise Science and has completed her Master's Degree in Clinical Counseling. She is always looking for opportunities to expand and improve her skills so that she can apply them to her personal training repertoire. She belongs to the international mentorship program Todd Durkin Mastermind Institute for Fitness Professionals, and in March 2018 was awarded the Todd Durkin Mastermind Institute Fitness Professional of the Year Award

Jenn is a mother of two boys and enjoys an active lifestyle. She is currently training for Triathlons and will be travelling to various races in Alberta and British Columbia this year to expand her triathlon experiences. She enjoys snowboarding, paddle boarding, kayaking, and hiking

Whether you work with Jenn in a small group or one-on-one, you will find that she is capable of modifying your workout to your specific fitness goals. Her philosophy of 1% better every day provides a supportive relationship with her clients in moving forward and continually improving body and mind to achieve success

Chapter 8

It's Never Too Late

By Kelli O'Brien Watson

The amazing thing isn't that he came in 2nd place in the Master's Division of the triathlon. It was that, until he turned 49 years old, he had never exercised a day in his life. His story is the perfect example that it is never too late to try something new or to compete as an athlete.

As he neared his 50th birthday, Mark made a decision. He wanted to lose the extra 40 pounds of weight he had gained over the past few years. He wanted to start his next decade lighter and healthier. He talked to some friends, did some research, and decided he would accomplish his goal by running.

He had never run.

In fact, he had never exercised. He worked his way through high school and didn't have time to play sports. So, this was his first venture into any kind of exercise.

You can imagine how that went.

When he first came to me, several months later, he was running 10 miles a day! He had turned 50. He had lost 20 pounds. But now his knees hurt. His back hurt. And he was frustrated that he wasn't losing any more weight.

We went through the assessments – postural analysis, functional movement screening, weight, body composition, and more. The end result was that he had some weak muscles, some tight muscles, some compensatory movement patterns and his weight and body composition were both higher than he wanted them to be. All of these issues, coupled with the over-use injuries from running without proper training, meant he was in pain – and stuck.

The best part was that he didn't want to give up. He had discovered a new hobby in exercise. He liked the discipline of it, and the way it made him feel. He liked having a goal that he could work toward, and now he wanted to see more results.

So, for the first time in his life, at 50 years old, he began a personal training program.

To his credit, he was consistent. He followed the plan. He ate right and exercised correctly. Because he did, he began to see those results. He put on several pounds of muscle and took off several pounds of fat. It wasn't long before his body composition went from 21% body fat to 12% and he dropped 25 pounds.

At this point, he felt so much better. He had more energy. He could do so much more. And he liked the way he looked. Although he weighed the same as he had weighed in high school, he now had a lot of muscle on his body. Everywhere he went people commented on how great he looked, and of course, that positive reinforcement fueled his desire to do even more.

As a personal trainer, I like to tell people I am in the business of "joint preservation." If we treat our joints well, we will continue to live a full and active life. Once our joints begin to fail, we stop moving, and that is the beginning of the slow decline in life.

With Mark's joints in mind, I suggested he try cycling. He had never really done much bicycling, even as a kid, but he was ready to try something new. He started on a stationary bike, but quickly learned that his attention span craved more stimulation. So, he bought a road bike and began to ride outside. He incorporated his bike rides into his exercise plan, found some fun apps on his phone to help him map out his routes, and discovered another hobby.

Miles of riding later, I suggested he might want to participate in The Ride for Missing Children – a 100-mile bike ride that raises money for programs through the National Center for Missing and Exploited Children. Although 100 miles seemed daunting to him, it wasn't a race. The event was a 'team ride' where everyone rides 2x2 at a steady pace for the entire distance. It required endurance, but not speed. It seemed like an opportune event to help him continue to challenge himself without going overboard.

Sure enough, he completed it with no problem. He felt great afterwards – not just because he could ride that distance, but because he could use his newly-discovered athletic abilities to help others. It was a whole new world for him, and he was excited about the opportunities he now had to make a difference. There were many local running and biking events to raise money for different charitable organizations, and he signed up and completed several of them that summer.

The next challenge came as winter emerged. He had to put his outdoor bike away and make a choice. Did he want to ride a stationary bike all winter? Or did he want to try another challenge?

True to himself – he wanted another challenge. So, I suggested he go to a local indoor pool and sign up to swim for the winter. When I suggested it, his face showed a mixture of excitement and dread. He had never been a swimmer. It was another thing he hadn't done much as a child and he knew he wasn't good at it. At the same time, he had a competitive streak in his nature, and he wanted to challenge himself.

Those first few weeks of swimming were very challenging. He had a lot of muscle on his body, and he wasn't a strong swimmer, so he tended to sink. That made it hard to get a rhythm in his strokes and his breathing. We slowed him down and spent some time in the shallow end working on fundamentals. He also got better equipment and learned that goggles can make a huge difference. It wasn't long before he began to see progress. Slowly, he began to improve his endurance. Before long he was swimming twice a week and improving steadily.

When spring came, he wanted to know what was next. As usual, he was ready for another challenge and wanted to know his options. We recognized that he now had all the components to be able to compete in a triathlon, so I asked what he thought of that idea. It was a big step, but I was confident he had what it took to do it. He agreed, and a new training plan emerged.

The most challenging part of working with Mark was keeping him challenged without letting him over-do it. His competitive nature made him want to go-go-go, and he struggled with taking days off. I kept reiterating this simple point – recovery is part of the workout. In fact, recovery is the most important piece of the workout. Without it, you end up breaking down, instead of building up. With preservation of the joints in mind, recovery is an important part of that process.

The best part of working with him was his dedication and consistency. He did everything he was told. He followed the plan to a T. He worked hard, and he did it the right way. That is why, when the triathlon came in May, he was able to complete it. It wasn't easy. There were issues with his wet suit, the weather was cold and damp and his muscles tightened up because of it, and there were times on the run when he didn't think he would finish. But he did. And he learned a lot in the process.

Once he recovered, he told me he wanted to do another one to see if he could improve. And sure enough, that led to a series of triathlons over the next few years. Each time, he learned something more, and he improved. Eventually, he started getting close to placing in his age group – the Master's Division – and that inspired him to try even harder. He wanted to be in the top three.

We periodized his training program, dialed in his nutrition, and worked on improving the areas that challenged him. He enjoyed every minute. He enjoyed the discipline, the structure, and he especially enjoyed seeing the results.

That was when he started placing in the events, first 3rd, then 2nd. Of course, he is still striving for first. Most importantly, however, is that in his late 50s, he is now an accomplished triathlete.

Although I love to share success stories, that isn't the only reason I'm sharing this one. You see, I often hear people say, "I'm too old," or "It's too late for me," and I believe that is simply a state of mind. I am not suggesting that anyone can or will become a triathlete, but I am suggesting that if you set your mind to something, you can accomplish it.

Here is all you need:

A Decision

If you want to improve your life, start by deciding to improve your health. It's a choice. You can either sit still or you can get moving. You can either eat well or not. You can either challenge yourself or you can be lazy. The choice is yours. But the first step – a decision to change – can put you on a path to things you might never have even imagined.

People

You don't need to do it alone. In fact, it's better to find professionals who can help you. Not only will it ensure you are doing things properly, but you can get injured if you're not careful. Find a trainer and let them guide you. It will keep you accountable as well as safe.

Perseverance

It isn't easy to do anything new. It is challenging, and it can also be frustrating. Giving up is an easy out. But if you keep striving to improve and are willing to learn, then you will enjoy the experience. And if you enjoy it, you will keep coming back for more.

So where is Mark now?

Still striving. Still competing. And becoming better at recovering.

He has increased the distance of his triathlons. He has a 10% body composition in his late 50s, and he weighs what he did in high school. He continues to set high goals for himself and would like to come in 1st in an event at some point. I'm sure he will.

Ultimately, though, he is an absolutely great example of my belief that, "It's never too late."

About Kelli O'Brien Watson

Kelli O'Brien Watson is a best-selling author, coach, presenter and the owner of Studio 8 Academy, an online holistic wellness center. Recently, she co-founded Scriptor Publishing Group, Inc., a publishing company dedicated to helping fitness professionals share their stories and publish their books.

Kelli holds a Master's Degree in Counseling Education and certifications in Personal Training, TRX and Youth Fitness. She is the author of *Kelli's Quips: Happy Thoughts for Busy People* and *Finding My Way Back to Me: A Journey of Self-Discovery.* She has also co-authored several books, including, most recently, the Amazon best-seller, *Author University*.

She is a Platinum Level Coach for the Todd Durkin Mastermind Group, where she provides business and personal development coaching for fitness professionals around the world. She also runs a life coaching program called *Finding My Way Back to Me*.

Kelli is the recipient of the Accent on Excellence Award for her work throughout her community, and she presents, locally and nationally, on topics having to do with health, wellness, mindset and performance. In 2013, she was honored to be a presenter for the first TedXUtica program.

Kelli's life purpose is to help people get stronger – inside and out, and she does that with enthusiasm in whatever she pursues. However, she finds her greatest joy in the time spent with her family – Graeme, Marcus, Caitlin, Katie, Cameron, and Kira – and their completely loveable, dog, Cody.

WANT TO BE A PUBLISHED AUTHOR?

Scriptor Publishing Group offers services including writing, publishing, marketing and consulting to take your book…

From Dream to Published!

Email us at
info@scriptorpublishinggroup.com
to get started!

36960621R00087

Made in the USA
Lexington, KY
19 April 2019